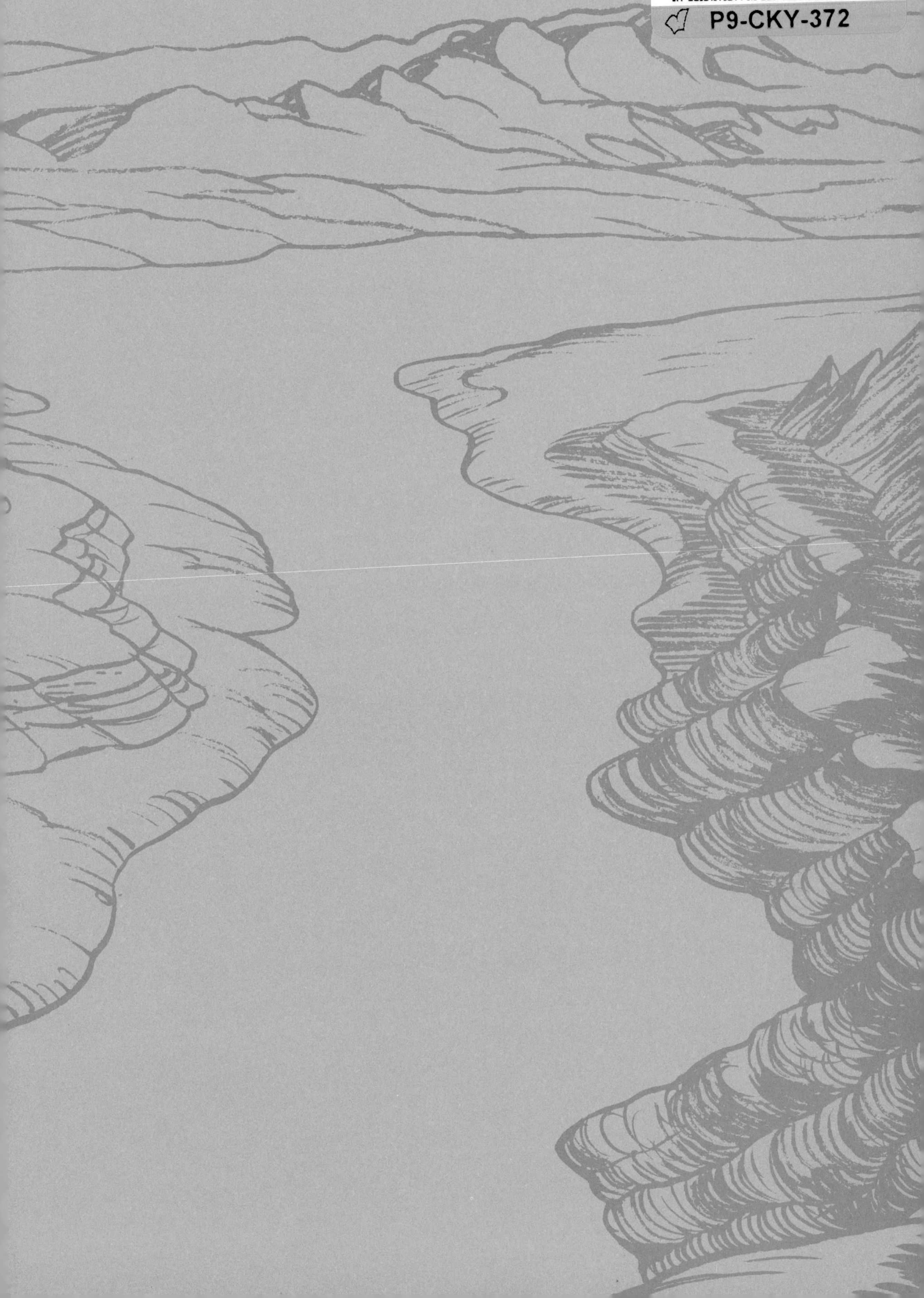

Frederik Peeters

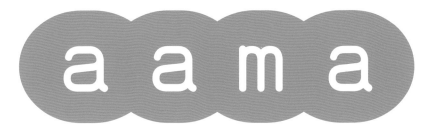

1. The Smell of Warm Dust

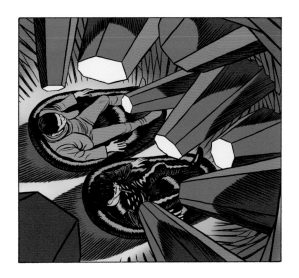

SELF MADE HERO

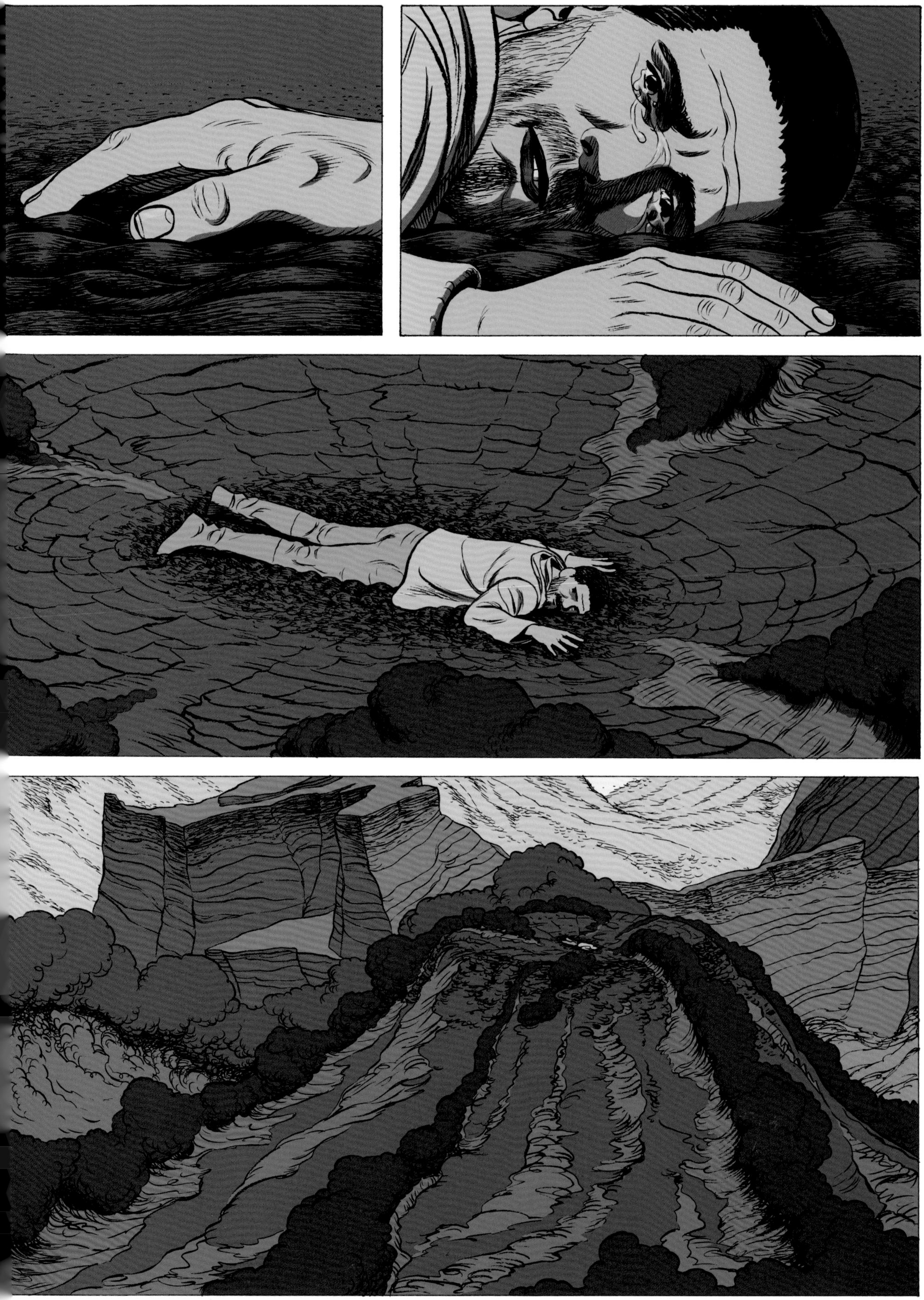

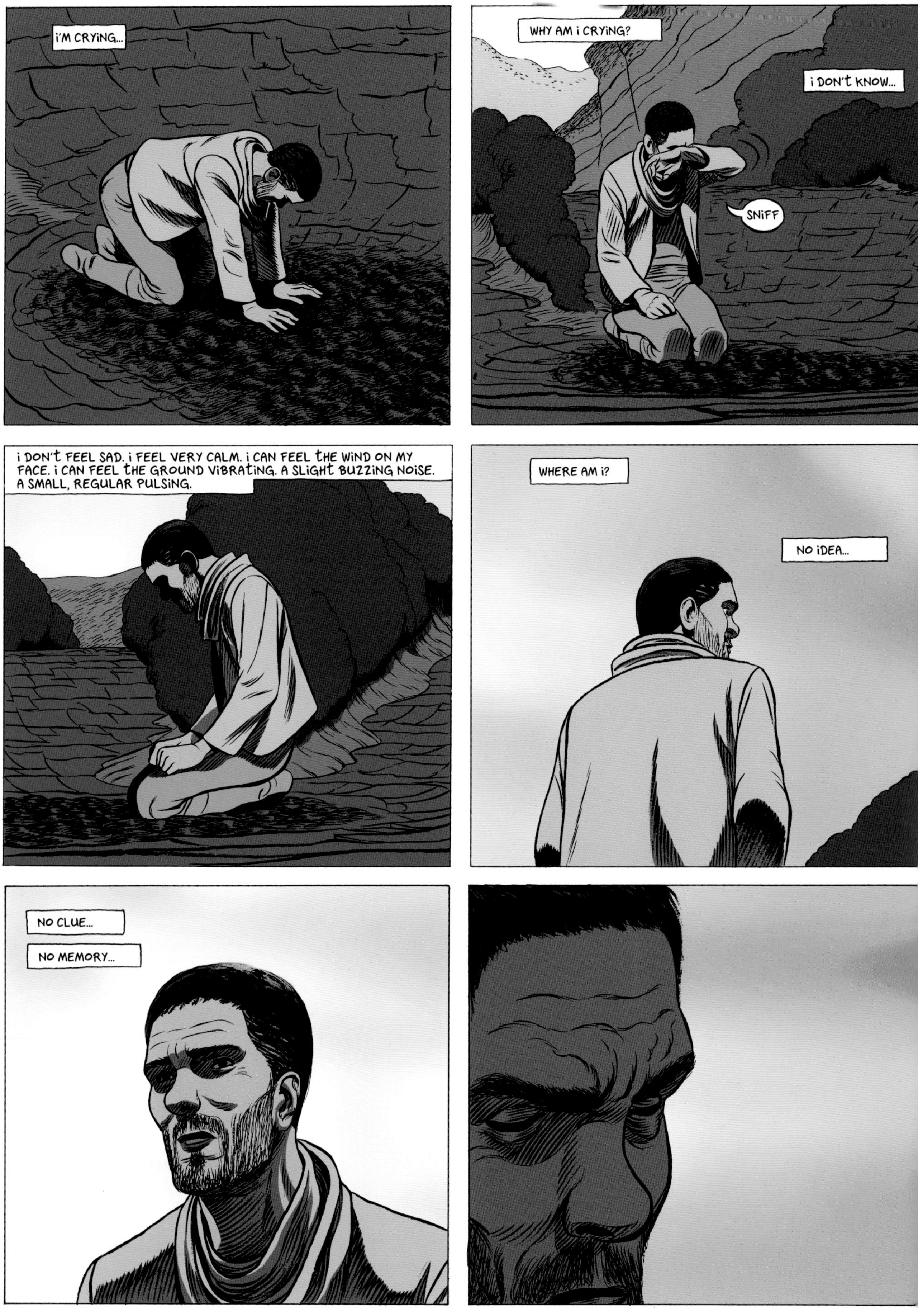

i'M CRYiNG...
WHY AM i CRYiNG?
i DON'T KNOW...
SNiFF
i DON'T FEEL SAD. i FEEL VERY CALM. i CAN FEEL THE WiND ON MY FACE. i CAN FEEL THE GROUND ViBRATiNG. A SLiGHT BUZZiNG NOiSE. A SMALL, REGULAR PULSiNG.
WHERE AM i?
NO iDEA...
NO CLUE...
NO MEMORY...

LILJA...

ANYTHING ELSE?

YES...

MY GIRL...
MY LITTLE DAUGHTER.

NO...

NOTHING.

I'M EMPTY... COMPLETELY CLEANED OUT. IT'S LIKE THE TEARS HAVE WASHED EVERYTHING AWAY...

THAT'S IT.

SOMEONE!

SOMEONE'S COMING!

THAT WAY...

I CAN SEE CLEARLY. MY VISION IS PERFECTLY CLEAR! SO CLEAR IT ALMOST HURTS MY EYES... THAT'S NOT NORMAL. I'M NEARSIGHTED, RIGHT?

YEAH... NORMALLY I'M NEARSIGHTED.

VERLOC! WONDERFUL!

YOU'RE ALIVE!

VERLOC!

MY NAME!

MY NAME IS VERLOC...

HELLO, MY NAME IS VERLOC.

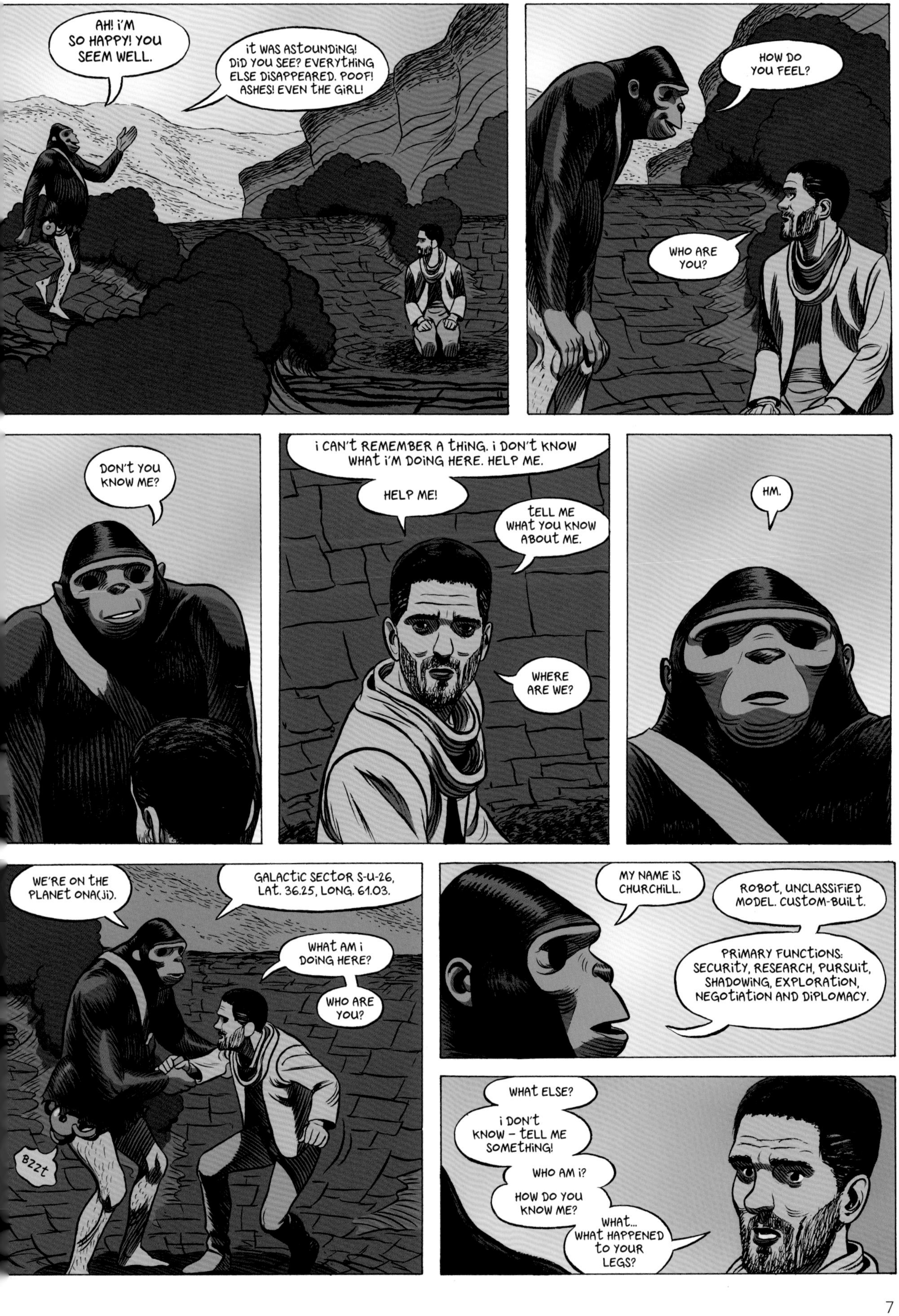
AH! i'M SO HAPPY! YOU SEEM WELL.
it WAS ASTOUNDiNG! DiD YOU SEE? EVERYTHiNG ELSE DiSAPPEARED. POOF! ASHES! EVEN tHE GiRL!
HOW DO YOU FEEL?
WHO ARE YOU?
DON'T YOU KNOW ME?
i CAN'T REMEMBER A tHiNG. i DON'T KNOW WHAt i'M DOiNG HERE. HELP ME.
HELP ME!
tELL ME WHAt YOU KNOW ABOUt ME.
WHERE ARE WE?
HM.
WE'RE ON tHE PLANEt ONA(Ji).
GALACtiC SECtOR S-U-26, LAt. 36.25, LONG. 61.03.
WHAt AM i DOiNG HERE?
WHO ARE YOU?
BZZt
MY NAME iS CHURCHiLL.
ROBOt, UNCLASSiFiED MODEL. CUSTOM-BUiLt.
PRiMARY FUNCtiONS: SECURity, RESEARCH, PURSUit, SHADOWiNG, EXPLORAtiON, NEGOtiAtiON AND DiPLOMACY.
WHAt ELSE?
i DON'T KNOW – tELL ME SOMEtHiNG!
WHO AM i?
HOW DO YOU KNOW ME?
WHAt... WHAt HAPPENED tO YOUR LEGS?

MAYBE WE SHOULD GET BACK TO THE COLONY. I'LL SEE IF COMMUNICATIONS ARE BACK UP...

Z...

NO! I WANT TO KNOW!

RIGHT NOW!

ONE MOMENT.

HERE.

WHAT'S THAT?

YOUR MEMOIRS.

OR A GOOD PORTION OF THEM, ANYWAY.

IS THIS A... BOOK?

MADE OF PAPER?

REAL PAPER...

SMELLS LIKE CHILDHOOD.

I KNOW THIS NOTEBOOK.

YES.

THIS IS MY HANDWRITING.

WHAT A STRANGE SENSATION...

OK... PAGE ONE.

IT SAYS:

MONDAY, JUNE 25.
TODAY IS A GREAT DAY! I'VE BEEN CARRYING THIS BLANK NOTEBOOK AROUND FOR MONTHS, SWEARING I'D SET DOWN MY THOUGHTS, OR THE DAY'S EVENTS, EVEN GROCERY LISTS OR WHAT HAVE YOU, AND TILL NOW I HAVEN'T BEEN ABLE TO WRITE A WORD.

NOW IT'S EASY ALL OF A SUDDEN! I SIT DOWN, GRAB A PEN — A REAL PEN, WITH REAL INK — AND WRITE... GOOD GRIEF, IT'S BEEN SO LONG. EVEN AT SCHOOL, I DON'T REMEMBER WRITING BY HAND LIKE THIS. WELL, I MEAN, JUST LOOK AT IT, IT'S PATHETIC; I HAVE THE HANDWRITING OF A SEVEN YEAR OLD.

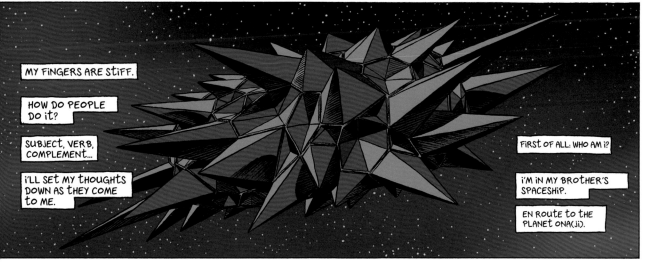

MY FINGERS ARE STIFF.

HOW DO PEOPLE DO IT?

SUBJECT, VERB, COMPLEMENT...

I'LL SET MY THOUGHTS DOWN AS THEY COME TO ME.

FIRST OF ALL: WHO AM I?

I'M IN MY BROTHER'S SPACESHIP.

EN ROUTE TO THE PLANET ONA(JI).

BEHIND ME IS CHURCHILL. WE JUST TALKED FOR AN HOUR. WELL, I DID MOST OF THE TALKING. IT ALL CAME TUMBLING OUT IN ASTONISHING DISARRAY. I TRIED TO RECALL THE CIRCUMSTANCES LEADING UP TO THAT PUDDLE WHERE THEY FOUND ME — HE AND MY BROTHER.

FOR A MOMENT, I SAW MYSELF FROM THE OUTSIDE, BEING PSYCHOANALYZED BY AN APE. AMUSING, TO SAY THE LEAST.

I DON'T KNOW IF I DID THE RIGHT THING, AGREEING TO THIS TRIP. WELL... OF COURSE. ONE WAY OR ANOTHER, SOMETHING HAD TO GIVE. STILL, FLEEING TO THE FAR END OF THE GALAXY WON'T EXACTLY HELP ME SEE MY DAUGHTER AGAIN.

NOW...

PERHAPS A BIT OF ORDER.

WHY AM I HERE?

WE SET OFF FROM RADIANT EIGHTEEN HOURS AGO.

RADIANT.

THE NIGHT BEFORE LAST, THEN... THE PUDDLE. LET'S START WITH THE PUDDLE. SHIT, I WAS SO WASTED! I WAS COMING OFF A BENDER AT TAFFY'S SHIA, MY LONGEST EVER. TEN HOURS, MAYBE TWELVE... EVEN FIFTEEN.

FIFTEEN HOURS STEWING IN SHIA, BLOWING MY LAST CREDITS.

MY BLOOD MUST'VE BEEN THICKER THAN MOTOR OIL.

I COULD'VE DIED WITH A SMILE ON MY FACE. COMPLETELY BLISSED OUT, MISTAKING DEATH FOR A BILLBOARD.

THAT WAS WHEN MY BROTHER SPOKE MY NAME. HIS VOICE HELD A VAGUE HINT OF REPROACH.

VERLOC?!

I REMEMBER, WEIRDLY, THINKING OF MY OLD BIOTECH PROF, WHO USED TO TELL ME:

VERLOC NIM,

YOU'RE JUST A PIECE OF SHIT ON A TOOTHPICK!

VERLOC?!

IS THAT YOU?

MY LITTLE BROTHER, WHOM I HADN'T SEEN FOR... WHAT, TEN YEARS? YEAH, SINCE DAD DIED...

MY LITTLE BROTHER...

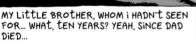

...WHO WAS A LITTLE PRICK.

STILL, I WAS GLAD TO SEE HIM.

JUST LOOK AT YOURSELF!

ARE YOU OK?

CONRAD?

CONRAD!

WHAT A COINCIDENCE, SEEING YOU HERE!

WHAT THE FUCK ARE YOU DOING ON LEVEL 1?

COME FOR THE WHORES, HAVE YOU?

I CAN SMELL THE SHIA ON YOU FROM A MILE OFF!

SHIA AND SHIT!

PLEASANT AS EVER.

SHOULD I GET A DOCTOR?

UH... NO, DEFINITELY NOT. NO DOCTORS, NO POLICE.

C'MON, LET'S WALK.

I HAVE TO WALK!

HA HA, THIS IS CRAZY, BUT I'M ALMOST HAPPY TO SEE YOU! WHO'S THE GUY DRESSED AS A GORILLA?

THAT'S CHURCHILL, A ROBOT. MY BODYGUARD, IN A WAY.

HEYA, CHURCHILL. WHAT'S THE HAPS?

A PLEASURE, SIR.

A BODYGUARD! SO, YOU'VE GONE AND BECOME IMPORTANT, EH? POLITICS? FINANCE? FEMTOTECH?

MM... AND YOU? YOU'RE QUITE THE MAN OF MYSTERY.

STILL LIVING OFF DAD'S BOUTIQUE?

NAH.

NOT NOW.

'S'A LONG STORY.

SHIT, VERLOC, HAVE YOU SEEN YOURSELF? SORRY, BUT YOU LOOK LIKE A DREG FROM LEVEL 1! WHAT HAPPENED TO YOU?

DON'T TELL ME YOU LIVE HERE?

CRAP, YOUR FACE IS COVERED WITH STAINS!

OH, THAT WAS SOMETHING ELSE. I LOST MY PHARYNGEAL FILTER. TOOK IT ALL OUT TEN YEARS AGO.

NO MORE EYE IMPLANTS! NO MORE CEREBROTEL, EVEN! NOT A GENEMOD ON ME!

LONG LIVE FREEDOM!

RIIIIGHT... YOU'RE A REGULAR PUROGENE.

HA HA HA! NO WAY! PUROGENES ARE OPINIONATED, BIGOTED AND DELIBERATELY HOSTILE!

NOT MY TYPE AT ALL!

MM... OF COURSE NOT.

AND LILJA AND SILIKA?

WHAT ABOUT 'EM?

WELL, I MEAN... HOW ARE THEY?

HMPH! SILIKA AND I BROKE UP THIRTEEN MONTHS AGO. I HAVE NO RIGHT TO SEE LILJA ANY MORE.

SO WHILE I'D REALLY LIKE TO ANSWER YOUR QUESTION, I CAN'T.

SO BASICALLY YOU'VE GOT A BLACK EYE, YOUR SKIN'S HALF-MAUVE, AND YOU LOST DAD'S STORE AND YOUR WIFE AND KID.

PLUS I HAVEN'T A DIME TO MY NAME, WHICH SHOULD CERTAINLY TICKLE YOUR INCORRIGIBLE SENSE OF SUPERIORITY WHERE I'M CONCERNED.

YOU'RE IN DEEP SHIT, THEN.

THAT'S IT! I'M IN DEEP SHIT!

THE BLACKEST SHIT!

UP TO MY NECK!

HA HA HA!!

IT'S A TOTAL DISASTER!

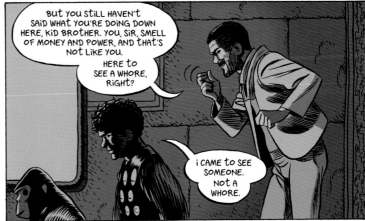

BUT YOU STILL HAVEN'T SAID WHAT YOU'RE DOING DOWN HERE, KID BROTHER. YOU, SIR, SMELL OF MONEY AND POWER, AND THAT'S NOT LIKE YOU.

HERE TO SEE A WHORE, RIGHT?

I CAME TO SEE SOMEONE. NOT A WHORE.

HMPH! I DON'T REALLY KNOW WHERE WE ARE, BUT IF YOU KEEP GOING DOWN THAT WAY, WE'LL REACH THE INHABITED NECROPOLIS, AND I—

WE'RE ALREADY THERE, VERLOC.

AH.

YOU KNOW WHAT THEY SAY ABOUT THE INHABITED NECROPOLIS, RIGHT?

WE'LL BE FINE WITH CHURCHILL.

IT WASN'T JUST THE FACT OF SEEING MY BROTHER THAT FLIPPED A SWITCH IN ME.

BEEP

IT'S ME. CONRAD.

ARF

NOR WAS IT OUR SUDDENLY SHOWING UP IN THE DISTRICT OF THE DEAD, WHICH I'D ALWAYS CAREFULLY AVOIDED FROM SUPERSTITION.

NO, THE MOMENT I FELT A DOOR SWING OPEN INSIDE ME, ALMOST BODILY...

HELLO, MY FRIEND!

...WAS WHEN I RECOGNIZED HIM.

HOW ARE YOU?

YOU LOOK WELL!

LOOK WHO I RAN INTO BY ACCIDENT! GOOD OLD VERLOC, REMEMBER?

HA HA, DELIGHTED! I...

EXCUSE ME. LET ME GET A BIT CLOSER, I'M VERY NEARSIGHTED.

ELIAS?!

MY BROTHER GAVE ME A LOOK THAT SAID: "ACT LIKE NOTHING'S WRONG. I'LL EXPLAIN LATER!"

WELL, FANCY THAT!

WHAT A DAY FOR REUNIONS, RIGHT?

HA HA...

ARF!

UM...

WELL... I WAS JUST DROPPING BY TO SEE IF EVERYTHING WAS OK.

IS MRS CASTILLO STILL SEEING TO MEALS AND CLEANING?

RR...

ARF...

MY OWN WRETCHEDNESS PRACTICALLY LEAPT OUT AT ME...

I MAY BE GOING AWAY FOR A WHILE. POSSIBLY ON A LONG MISSION...

SO I BROUGHT YOU MORE MONEY THAN USUAL. BUT YOU HAVE TO SPEND IT CAREFULLY.

SLRP...

...INTENSIFIED BY ASTONISHMENT AT SEEING MY BROTHER BEHAVE IN A WAY TOTALLY CONTRARY TO MY IMAGE OF HIM.

MY OWN WRETCHEDNESS...

MY INABILITY TO TAKE CARE OF MY OWN FAMILY...

AND MY INTENSE LONELINESS.

(C'MON. LET'S GO.)

BYE!

UH... TILL NEXT TIME!

CALL ME WHENEVER, OK?

SHIT! WAS THAT REALLY ELIAS?

WHAT HAPPENED TO HIM?

SIGH...

ELIAS HAD BEEN MY BROTHER'S BEST FRIEND IN HIGH SCHOOL. DESPITE WHAT I'D THOUGHT, THEY'D STAYED IN TOUCH, IF DISTANTLY, HE EXPLAINED. ELIAS HAD BECOME A HISTORY OF HUMANITY PROFESSOR, AND HE'D OFTEN AFFECTIONATELY QUESTIONED CONRAD'S PROFESSIONAL CHOICES. AND THEN, LIKE SO MANY OTHERS, HE WAS SWEPT AWAY IN THE GREAT CRISIS, WHEN TEACHING HISTORY BECAME AN ABSTRACT LUXURY. HE LOST EVERYTHING HE HAD.

HE LANDED ON LEVEL 1, GOT A TERRIBLE CASE OF BERN'S DISEASE, AND COULDN'T PAY FOR GENETIC CORRECTION. BY THE TIME CONRAD FOUND OUT, IT WAS TOO LATE.

HE'LL DEFINITELY DIE. BUT MEANWHILE, I TRY TO DO WHAT I CAN.

THIS IS ALL TO YOUR CREDIT.

SPIT

IT'S JUST TOO BAD YOU NEVER HAD THE SAME NOBILITY OF SPIRIT WHEN IT CAME TO DAD.

SHUT UP, VERLOC!

I DON'T LIKE MYSELF WHEN I'M LIKE THIS.

VERLOC NIM!

STOP! DON'T MOVE!

SHIT!

WHAT'S WRONG?

HURRY! LET'S GO!

WAIT! IS THAT THE POLICE?

NO, THEY'RE PRIVATE SECURITY. THEY'RE IN CHARGE OF MAKING SURE I DON'T SEE MY DAUGHTER!

HMPH...

STAY WHERE YOU ARE!

TYPE B NEUTRALIZATION. MAKE SURE WE'RE NOT FOLLOWED, AND MEET US AT THE SHIP.

UNDERSTOOD.

THIS WAY!

HA HA! YOU'RE IN TROUBLE NOW, LITTLE BROTHER!

YOU THINK?

NOT WITH PRIVATE SECURITY. I'M ABOVE THAT.

PANT WAIT!

PANT

EASY NOW...

SIT DOWN!

WOW! I'VE NEVER SEEN ANYTHING LIKE THIS!

GUESS IT'S NOT HARD TIMES FOR EVERYONE.

SO IT'S TRUE.

YOU REALLY ARE IMPORTANT.

WHAT'S THIS MISSION YOU WERE TALKING ABOUT?

I WORK FOR THE MUY-TANG CORPORATION.

THE BIOROBOTICS COMPANY?

THAT'S RIGHT.

SHIT, CONRAD...

THEY'RE ONE OF THE COMPANIES BEHIND THE GREAT CRISIS!

BEEP BEEP

THEY'RE WHY ELIAS LIVES AMONG THE DEAD! AND YOU W—

NOT NOW, VERLOC, NOT NOW. WE CAN HAVE THIS CONVERSATION LATER, IF YOU WANT.

WHAT DO YOU DO FOR THEM?

I KEEP THE WHEELS GREASED, YOU MIGHT SAY. I TRAVEL THE GALAXY SOLVING SMALL COMMUNICATIONS ISSUES.

RIIIIGHT...

WHICH MEANS WHAT?

WHICH MEANS... I SPY, NEGOTIATE, TWIST ARMS AND TAKE CARE OF LOOSE ENDS.

CALL IT THE DEVIL'S WORK, BUT INDIRECTLY WHAT I DO SAVES MILLIONS OF LIVES.

IN A FEW HOURS, I'M HEADED FOR THE FAR REACHES OF SPACE, TO ONA(JI), THE LAST INHABITABLE PLANET DISCOVERED. ONA(JI)'S IN A DEVELOPMENTAL STAGE LIKE THAT OF A PRIMITIVE EARTH, CIRCA THE CAMBRIAN ERA.

FIVE YEARS AGO, MUY-TANG SENT OUT A SMALL SCIENTIFIC EXPEDITION UNDER PROFESSOR WOLAND. SHE'S JUST PERFECTED A REVOLUTIONARY TECHNOLOGY, A KIND OF SOUP OF NETWORKED PICO-ROBOTS. THEY CAN REPRODUCE, AND ALSO MANIPULATE AND TRANSFORM MATTER AT A SUBATOMIC LEVEL.

I DIDN'T CATCH A WORD OF THAT.

YOU'RE BETTER OFF. AT LEAST THIS WAY YOU WON'T TELL ANYONE.

FACT IS, WOLAND WAS SUPPOSED TO USE ONA(JI)'S PRIMITIVE LIFE TO MAKE A BIG SHOW OF HOW POWERFUL HER INVENTION WAS, THUS ASSURING MUY-TANG'S MARKET SUPREMACY FOR THE NEXT FIFTY YEARS.

BUT?

BUT...

THE GREAT CRISIS HAPPENED. THE COMPANY DRASTICALLY SLASHED ITS BUDGET, INCLUDING WOLAND'S PROGRAMME.

SOON IT'LL BE SIX YEARS SINCE THE COLONISTS WERE LEFT ON THEIR OWN. FINANCES ARE A BIT MORE STABLE NOW, SO IT'S VITAL THAT THE COMPANY RECOVER WOLAND AND HER MIRACLE PRODUCT.

THAT'S WHERE I COME IN. MY MISSION.

I DON'T REALLY KNOW WHAT TO THINK OF ALL THIS.

YOU TALK LIKE A BANKER...

YOU SHOULD COME WITH ME.

HA HA HA HA HA HA

HAHA

I'M SERIOUS, VERLOC!

I WON'T INSIST, BUT IT'D CLEAR YOUR HEAD.

IT'D BE A BREATH OF FRESH AIR.

CONRAD'S INVITATION WAS TINGED WITH A MIXTURE OF PITY AND AFFECTION...

I HATE PITY.

BUT I SAID YES.

I COULD'VE SAID SOMETHING LIKE: "LISTEN, KIDDO, I DON'T NEED YOUR PITY!" BUT I HAD TO ADMIT THAT NOT NEEDING ANYONE HAD LEFT ME ALL ALONE IN THE WORLD.

BESIDES, SOMETHING HAD CLICKED INSIDE ME. IT'S STILL HARD TO BELIEVE MY BROTHER WAS REALLY TRYING TO DO ME A FAVOUR, BUT I'LL FIND OUT SOON ENOUGH.

I'M GOING TO STOP WRITING FOR NOW.

MY HAND HURTS.

WHAT'S TODAY'S DATE?

3 JULY.

SEVEN DAYS...

SEVEN DAYS SINCE I STARTED WRITING.

SNIFF

FLIP

TUES, 26 JUNE.

I SLEEP. THAT'S ALL I DO.

JUST NOW I WAS BRIEFLY AWAKE. I STOPPED IN FRONT OF A WINDOW, CAPTIVATED BY WHAT I GUESS WAS THE STARRY VOID, WITHOUT REALLY UNDERSTANDING WHAT I WAS SEEING. THIS IS THE FIRST TIME I'VE EVER BEEN OUT THIS FAR.

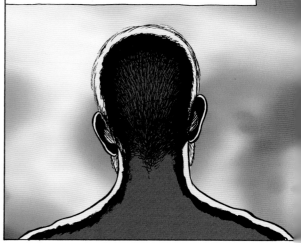

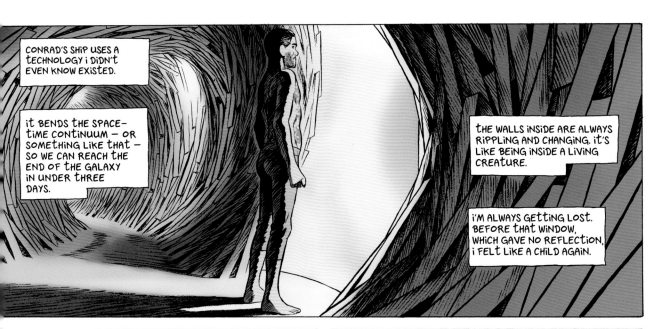

CONRAD'S SHIP USES A TECHNOLOGY I DIDN'T EVEN KNOW EXISTED.

IT BENDS THE SPACE-TIME CONTINUUM — OR SOMETHING LIKE THAT — SO WE CAN REACH THE END OF THE GALAXY IN UNDER THREE DAYS.

THE WALLS INSIDE ARE ALWAYS RIPPLING AND CHANGING. IT'S LIKE BEING INSIDE A LIVING CREATURE.

I'M ALWAYS GETTING LOST. BEFORE THAT WINDOW, WHICH GAVE NO REFLECTION, I FELT LIKE A CHILD AGAIN.

MY BODY'S GOING THROUGH A SPRING CLEANING: SORTING OUT THE SHIA, DISCARDING EXTRANEOUS STUFF. THE INCURABLE PESSIMIST INSIDE ME IS SLOWLY WAKING UP.

THE LIGHT, SWEET ATMOSPHERE HERE IS A NICE CHANGE FROM THE UNSTABLE GASES OF RADIANT'S LOWER LEVELS. I CAN BREATHE BETTER. MY USUAL FAINT MIGRAINE IS GONE.

THE WEIRDEST PART IS THAT I HAD A DREAM!

IT'S BEEN MONTHS SINCE I HAD ONE.

I'M WRITING IT DOWN BEFORE IT GOES AWAY.

IT STARTS WITH SILIKA STANDING BY A LAKE. I KNOW IT'S HER, THOUGH HER FACE IS INVISIBLE. BESIDE HER SITS LILJA IN AN OLD WOMAN'S BODY.

i GET CLOSER. SILIKA'S MUTTERING SOMETHING. SHE TURNS TOWARD ME. i KNOW SHE'S MOANING ABOUT LILJA'S PROBLEMS.

LILJA'S A LITTLE GIRL AGAIN. SILIKA PUTS A SHEET OVER HER FACE.

THE NEXT MINUTE, WE'RE BOTH RUNNING ACROSS AN ENORMOUS GRASSY PLAIN. SILIKA IS YELLING AT ME.

IT'S YOUR FAULT. YOUR FAULT!

THE GRASS IS REALLY SHARP AND CUTS MY FEET.

AN OLD BUILDING, FROM AN ANCIENT EARTH PAINTING, ADRIFT IN THE MIDDLE OF THE SEA.

A BIG OPEN WINDOW. CURTAINS FLYING. SILIKA STARING OFF INTO THE DISTANCE.

I'M BEHIND HER, SITTING AT A TABLE, READING AN OLD PRINT NEWSPAPER. I DON'T KNOW HOW, THOUGH, SINCE I'M WEARING GLASSES WHICH ARE COVERED WITH SOME KIND OF THICK CREAM...

THE DREAM ENDS. I'M NINE YEARS OLD, ON A ROAD. THERE'S SOME ROADKILL AT MY FEET. I SCREAM IN DESPAIR.

ALL THIS IS CLEARLY A PARABLE OF MY SEPARATION. BUT IT'S GOT NOTHING TO DO WITH HARD FACTS. NO, IT'S NOT MY FAULT.

IT'S NOT THAT SIMPLE...

I GO BACK TO SLEEP.

MORE SLEEP...

WEDS, 27 JUNE.

TODAY, I'M MORE OR LESS BACK ON MY FEET.

MORNING.

TYPE 3.

BUT WHEN I GOT UP, CONRAD WAS FROZEN IN A STRANGE POSTURE.

WHAT'S HE UP TO?

SNAP

CHECKING FLIGHT DATA.

SHEESH! AM I GLAD I GOT MY IMPLANTS OUT!

THERE.

ALL SYSTEMS NORMAL.

BEEP

I'D FORGOTTEN CONRAD WAS OBSESSED WITH DENTAL HYGIENE. ALWAYS TOYING WITH A TOOTHBRUSH, PROBABLY WITHOUT REALIZING.

CHEW

 I DON'T REALLY REMEMBER OUR CHILDHOOD TOGETHER. JUST A LITTLE RITUAL WE HAD BETWEEN US.

 ALL CLEAR?

YUP.

 ALL CLEAN?

YEP. ALL GOOD.

 I WAS PARANOID THAT SOME LITTLE BOOGER WAS STICKING OUT OF MY NOSE. HE WAS AFRAID THAT FOOD WAS STUCK IN HIS TEETH.

IT WAS RIDICULOUS. I DID NOT BRING IT UP.

 FEELING BETTER?

MM... YEAH.

IT'LL DO.

 ARE YOU SORRY YOU CAME WITH ME?

SLURP

 NO. BUT THE FOG'S CLEARING FROM MY HEAD, AND THINGS I'D RATHER HAVE FORGOTTEN ARE COMING BACK.

THIS MORNING, I WOKE UP SEEING PARJAPATH'S FACE.

PARJAPATH, THAT BASTARD!

 YEAH, IT'S CALLED REAL LIFE, VERLOC!

SOONER OR LATER YOU LOOK YOUR MISTAKES IN THE EYE.

JUST THE KIND OF THING MY BROTHER WOULD SAY.

 I DON'T KNOW IF IT'S FROM WRITING EVERY DAY, BUT I FEEL LIKE CONFIDING SOME LESS-THAN-NOBLE INCIDENTS THAT USUALLY WOULD'VE GOTTEN STUCK IN MY THROAT.

LISTEN... YOU SHOULD KNOW...

THAT I DIDN'T JUST LOSE DAD'S STORE.

WHAT DO YOU MEAN?

27

WHAT I MEAN IS, I COULD'VE...

I SHOULD'VE AVOIDED IT.

BUT I GOT TAKEN FOR A RIDE.

LIKE SOME ROOKIE.

THIS IS GONNA BE GOOD!

THIS WAS, WHAT... SIX OR SEVEN MONTHS AGO?

I WAS STILL REELING FROM MY SEPARATION.

I WASN'T GOING TO THE STORE MUCH... THERE WERE TOO MANY BAD MEMORIES. THAT WAS WHERE SILIKA HAD TOLD ME SHE WAS LEAVING.

IT WAS ALSO WHERE I HAD LEARNED ABOUT LILJA, YEARS AGO. I NEVER FELT GOOD THERE. SO I SPENT MOST OF MY TIME IN SHIA CLUBS.

THAT WAS WHERE I MET HIM. THE PERFECT CROOK. I'M SO ASHAMED WHEN I THINK BACK ON IT.

IT WAS ALL SO OBVIOUS, PROBABLY PLANNED IN ADVANCE. AND I DIDN'T SEE IT COMING AT ALL.

ARGAND LIQUEUR, PLEASE.

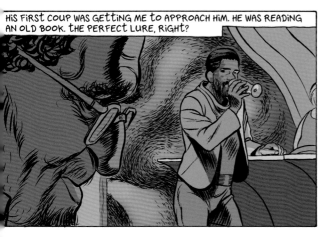

HIS FIRST COUP WAS GETTING ME TO APPROACH HIM. HE WAS READING AN OLD BOOK. THE PERFECT LURE, RIGHT?

EVENING.

SORRY TO BOTHER YOU, BUT—

NO, NO, PLEASE.

I WAS INTRIGUED BY WHAT YOU'VE GOT THERE.

SIT DOWN, YOUNG MAN.

THIS IS CALLED A PRINTED BOOK! IN A CERTAIN ERA—

YES, YES, I KNOW WHAT A BOOK IS!

I WAS JUST WONDERING WHAT KIND IT WAS...

MAY I?

BUT OF COURSE.

MAGNIFICENT!

HAND-SEWN BINDING...

CLOTH AND BOARD...

ANCIENT ARAB POETRY?

WELL, I'M IMPRESSED! IT'S HARD TO FIND A CONNOISSEUR LIKE YOU THESE DAYS!

PEOPLE USUALLY THINK I'M A CRAZY OLD MAN...

WELL, THAT MAKES TWO OF US.

DELIGHTED! MY NAME'S PARJAPATH.

VERLOC.

THE BOOK, TWO KINDRED SPIRITS WHO'D CHANCED UPON EACH OTHER: IT WAS SO WELL DONE.

WE TALKED TOGETHER FOR A LONG TIME.

NOW, I'M A MISTRUSTFUL FELLOW WITH A MISANTHROPIC STREAK, BUT...

PEOPLE DON'T KNOW HOW TO THINK ANY MORE. THEY'RE HYPNOTIZED BY EVERYTHING SHINY AND SHALLOW. NETWORKS, IMPLANTS — ALL THAT DISTRACTS US FROM THE TRUE BEAUTY AND UGLINESS OF LIFE...

EXACTLY!

COULDN'T PUT IT BETTER MYSELF.

BUT SOME PEOPLE KNOW HOW TO INSPIRE TRUST RIGHT OFF THE BAT, AND LIE WITH SUCH ASTONISHING EASE AND APLOMB. PEOPLE WHO CAN HIDE A DAGGER IN THE HAND THEY HOLD OUT.

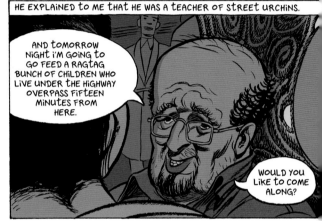

HE EXPLAINED TO ME THAT HE WAS A TEACHER OF STREET URCHINS.

AND TOMORROW NIGHT I'M GOING TO GO FEED A RAGTAG BUNCH OF CHILDREN WHO LIVE UNDER THE HIGHWAY OVERPASS FIFTEEN MINUTES FROM HERE.

WOULD YOU LIKE TO COME ALONG?

HE KNEW IT'D BE A WAY FOR ME TO SALVE MY CONSCIENCE.

SURE... WHY NOT?

I'M AFRAID I MUST BE GOING. I'VE A MEETING. LET'S MEET TOMORROW NIGHT AT NINE, SHALL WE?

PERHAPS YOU MIGHT BRING SOME MONEY — CASH — FOR FOOD?

HOW MUCH?

HOWEVER MUCH YOU FEEL IS RIGHT.

I'LL BE WAITING DOWN THERE.

SEE THAT LITTLE SQUARE ACROSS THE WAY WITH A TREE IN THE CORNER?

UM... NOT REALLY, NO. I'M NEAR-SIGHTED.

NO!

YOU TOO?!

WELL, THAT MAKES TWO OF US!

HAHA HAHAHA HAHA

A BIT LATER, I REALIZED EVEN THAT PART WAS CALCULATED.

OF COURSE, THE NEXT DAY THERE WERE NO STARVING CHILDREN, OR OVERPASSES.

HE SHOWED UP HALF AN HOUR LATER THAN PLANNED, LIMPING.

AH, VERLOC! YOU CAME!

I'M SO SORRY...

WHAT HAPPENED?

MEOW

OH, IT WAS SO STUPID OF ME. I BROKE MY BIG TOE AGAINST THE CURB.

HAVE A SEAT.

I HAD TO GO TO THE CLINIC.

IS IT BAD?

NO, BUT LET'S GO SEE THE CHILDREN ANOTHER TIME, SHALL WE?

NO PROBLEM.

DID YOU BRING THE MONEY?

YES.

GOOD.

VERY GOOD...

YOU'RE A GOOD MAN.

ALL THIS WAS JUST A PRETEXT TO SOFTEN ME UP AND TEST MY TRUST.

I CAN SHOW YOU MY SHOP, IF YOU'D LIKE.

IT'S NOT FAR. AND YOU'D LIKE IT, I'M SURE.

AH! YOU HAVE A SHOP?

WHAT KIND?

HIS SECOND COUP WAS THAT, UP TILL THEN, WE'D NEVER DISCUSSED THE STORE. EVEN THOUGH THAT'S WHAT HE WAS AFTER, HE ARRANGED THINGS SO THAT I BROUGHT IT UP FIRST.

YOU'LL SEE.

BUT I WANTED TO BUY YOU TEA TO APOLOGIZE.

I'LL MAKE US TEA AT THE SHOP.

IT WAS I WHO INVITED THE WOLF INTO THE FOLD! IN THE MIDDLE OF THE NIGHT!

KOGAKU 550DL

WHRR

CLICK!

HMM, A GENEPRINT LOCK! YOU MUST HAVE SOME REAL TREASURES IN HERE!

AND SINCE MY LIFE OF LATE SEEMED TO CONSIST OF A SERIES OF RUDE AWAKENINGS, I DIDN'T WAKE UP TILL THE WEE SMALL HOURS, WITH HIS GLASSES ON MY FACE...

IN A TOTALLY EMPTY STORE.

FINISH YOUR STORY!

WHAT'D HE DO?

OH, ISN'T IT OBVIOUS?

ONCE INSIDE, HE PLAYED UP HIS WONDER, WENT INTO CHILDISH RAPTURES...

HE FLATTERED ME...

I PREPARED US A POT OF MY BEST TEA.

E DISTRACTED ME BY ASKING IF E COULD EXAMINE A CERTAIN LLUSTRATED MAGAZINE FROM HE 21ST CENTURY.

OF COURSE. I HAVE A COPY IN VERY GOOD CONDITION!

THAT WAS WHEN HE MUST'VE SLIPPED SOMETHING INTO MY GLASS.

FEW MINUTES LATER, I BECAME IOLENTLY DIZZY.

POC

BEFORE GOING COMPLETELY UNDER, I SAW HIM LET A PARTNER IN. THEY TOOK IT ALL AWAY TOGETHER.

ALL I MANAGED WAS A GLIMPSE OF HIS SPITEFUL SATISFACTION WHEN HE BENT OVER AND PUT HIS GLASSES ON MY FACE...

I DIDN'T CATCH HIS LAST WORDS.

AND YOU NEVER TRIED TO FIND HIM?

I WANDERED AROUND TOWN ALL MORNING, CHEEKS FLUSHED. IF I'D FOUND HIM, I'D HAVE BEATEN HIS HEAD IN WITH MY BARE HANDS.

BUT I WAS DELUDING MYSELF. YOU KNOW PEOPLE LIKE HIM HAVE MASTERED POLYPLASTICITY.

AND THE COPS?

THE INSURANCE?

CONRAD... I WAS SO ASHAMED!

I SLEPT VERY POORLY FOR A LONG TIME. EVERY TRICK HE'D USED TO CON ME WOULD DANCE ENDLESSLY BEFORE MY EYES. ONLY THE SAD AND LONELY WOULD BE SO NAÏVE! HE'D REDUCED ME TO NOTHING. HE'D UNLEASHED SUCH A TORRENT OF RAGE, FRUSTRATION AND POWERLESSNESS INSIDE ME...

HE'D CLEANED ME OUT, WRUNG ME DRY, HUNG ME OUT LIKE AN OLD SOCK.

I'VE NEVER TOLD ANYONE THAT STORY...

I WAS EVEN RELIEVED DAD WASN'T AROUND TO TELL.

THE ARGUMENT THAT FOLLOWED ISN'T WORTH WRITING DOWN. WE'VE HAD IT HUNDREDS OF TIMES BEFORE. I HAVE AN AMBITIOUS, ARROGANT BROTHER, BRIMMING WITH PRINCIPLES, BUT HE GETS MY BLOOD GOING, AND PART OF ME IS GRATEFUL FOR IT.

WE SHOULD START MOVING AGAIN.
?

WHERE'S MY BROTHER?

I THINK IT'D BE BETTER IF YOU KEPT READING YOUR NOTES.

I'VE DETECTED A CRAFT FROM RADIANT JUST ENTERING ORBIT.
WE'LL SOON HAVE COMPANY. I TURNED OFF OUR TRANSPONDERS, TO BE SAFE.

WE CAN'T STAY HERE.
WE HAVE TO GET BACK TO THE COLONY NOW.
FINE.

THURS, 28 JUNE.

SIR. WE'RE NEARING OUR DESTINATION.

THIS WAY, PLEASE.

COMING...

YOU CAN CALL ME VERLOC, YOU KNOW. "SIR" IS A BIT AWKWARD.

VERY WELL.

VERLOC.

WHERE ARE YOU TAKING ME?

THE SICKBAY.

AH. IS SOMETHING WRONG?

ONA(JI)'S ATMOSPHERE IS SLIGHTLY TOXIC. IN YOUR CONDITION, YOU WOULD EXPERIENCE INCREASING DISCOMFORT LEADING TO CERTAIN DEATH TWO OR THREE HOURS AFTER DISEMBARKING.

I MUST INSTALL A PHARYNGEAL FILTER.

WHAT?!?

ARE YOU KIDDING? NO WAY, BONZO! I WON'T HAVE THAT SHIT IN ME!

AND DON'T YOU TRY TO FORCE IT ON ME!

YOUR REACTION WAS FORESEEABLE... AND UNDERSTANDABLE.

WHAT ALTERNATIVE DO YOU SUGGEST?

WHAT... ALTERNATIVE?

UH.

I...

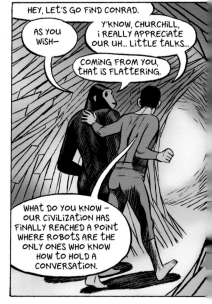

HEY, LET'S GO FIND CONRAD.

AS YOU WISH—

Y'KNOW, CHURCHILL, I REALLY APPRECIATE OUR UH... LITTLE TALKS...

COMING FROM YOU, THAT IS FLATTERING.

WHAT DO YOU KNOW — OUR CIVILIZATION HAS FINALLY REACHED A POINT WHERE ROBOTS ARE THE ONLY ONES WHO KNOW HOW TO HOLD A CONVERSATION.

OH, SPARE ME YOUR LUDDITE RANT, WILL YOU? DON'T START WITH THAT AGAIN.

IT'S A MATTER OF LIFE AND DEATH! IF YOU WANT, WE CAN PUT IN A TEMPORARY FILTER.

ONCE YOU'RE BACK, WE'LL TAKE IT OUT, AND YOU CAN SEE SPOTS AND GET MIGRAINES AGAIN.

NO WAY! MY BODY STAYS EXACTLY HOW IT IS!

HOW'D WE MANAGE BEFORE THEY STARTED GRAFTING THINGS ON TO US?

HOW'D THEY MANAGE IN THE EARLY DAYS OF SPACE EXPLORATION?

YOU KNOW, YOU ARE SOMETHING ELSE! DON'T YOU EVER LEARN A THING?

WE'RE LIVING IN THE HERE AND NOW.

THE GOLDEN AGE, TERRAN NOSTALGIA –

ALL THAT'S OVER!

HUMANS ARE JUST A BUNCH OF APES IN CLOTHES.

ONLY OUR CLOTHES KEEP US FROM RIPPING OUT EACH OTHER'S THROATS AND EATING EACH OTHER ALIVE.

THAT'S THE ONLY THING SEPARATING US FROM OUR PREHISTORIC ANCESTORS.

AND YOUR SPACETIME-DISTORTING VESSEL ISN'T GOING TO CHANGE THAT!

SIGH

AHEM.

FINE, FINE!

I PROBABLY HAVE AN ANCIENT-MODEL HELMET SOMEWHERE.

IF YOU FEEL LIKE COMPLICATING YOUR LIFE, CHURCHILL CAN FIND IT FOR YOU.

I HOPE YOU DIDN'T TAKE WHAT I SAID PERSONALLY. HM?

NO OFFENCE!

I DO NOT CONSIDER MYSELF AN APE, YOU KNOW.

NOTE TO SELF: I HAVE NOTHING AGAINST APES.

APES LIVE IN CONCRETE REALITY. I'D LIKE TO SAY AS MUCH FOR MY OWN LIFE.

SPEAKING OF WHICH, THE DESCENT TO ONA(JI) WAS OF UNEARTHLY BEAUTY.

I FEEL LIKE I'M STARTING MY LIFE OVER. THE WORRY IS GONE. I'M WIDE AWAKE...

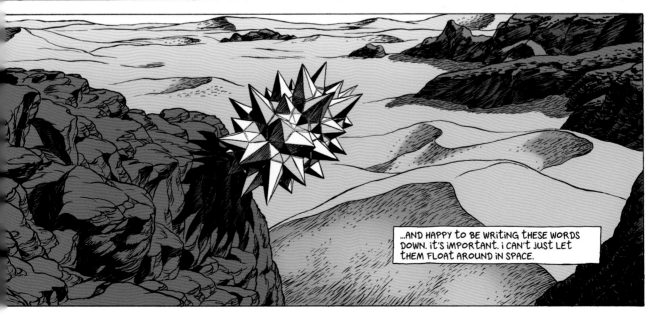

...AND HAPPY TO BE WRITING THESE WORDS DOWN. IT'S IMPORTANT. I CAN'T JUST LET THEM FLOAT AROUND IN SPACE.

MY ONLY MEMORIES OF TRAVEL ARE FROM A FEW TRIPS ON PUBLIC TRANSIT I TOOK ON THE MOON OF SEPHER TO SEE OUR GRANDMA. SEPHER IS SMALL, FLAT, DEVOID OF ATMOSPHERE, AND ALWAYS GREY.

IN CONTRAST, I HAVE NO WORDS TO DESCRIBE MY FIRST PHYSICAL CONTACT WITH ONA(JI). SOMETHING VAST AND PRIMAL THAT VIOLENTLY ROUSED ALL I FELT AS A CHILD, RAPT IN THE DIARIES OF EXPLORERS.

YOU OK?

HA HA!

I'M GREAT!

WONDERFUL!

UNREAL!

WATCH IT, VERLOC!

BE CAREFUL!

HAHA!

WELL....

THAT WAS SHORT.

STUPID MYOPIA!

KLAK

HURGGH

KOFF

AARGH!

KOFF

KOFF

HNNNGH!

ARRRRGH!

I'M DYING! DYYYING!

WHAT A MESS. WHAT A MESS!

WELL?

FEEL BETTER?

MMPH...

KOFF

SORRY

DON'T KNOW WHAT GOT INTO ME.

DON'T WORRY.

HAPPENS A LOT.

FIRST LANDINGS OFTEN CAUSE THAT KIND OF EUPHORIA.

YOU PUT A FILTER IN WHEN I WAS OUT COLD, DIDN'T YOU?

OF COURSE.

AND I KNOW YOU WON'T HAVE THE BALLS TO PROTEST AFTER WHAT HAPPENED!

AS A RESULT, THE SECOND ATTEMPT FELT MORE VIOLENT THAN THE FIRST, AS THE SMELLS OF WARM DUST, SULPHUR AND RUST ASSAULTED MY NOSTRILS. THE AROMA OF ADVENTURE.

AND THE SILENCE!

WHAT NOW?

WHAT'S NEXT ON THE AGENDA?

THE POD WE'RE SUPPOSED TO RECOVER HAS A GEO-TRANSPONDER. WORKS FINE. I'M GETTING A SIGNAL RIGHT NOW.

WE FIND THE POD AND GO HOME. SIMPLE.

IT'S GOING TO RAIN SOON.

IN 69 SECONDS.

OH WELL.

MOVE ON.

WE HAVE TO GET OUT OF THIS GORGE.

HERE! AN UMBRELLA!

GOT NOTHING AGAINST THOSE, I HOPE.

IS IT FAR?

JUST OVER AN HOUR'S WALK. THAT'S WHERE THE COLONY IS.

AN HOUR? WHY CAN'T WE JUST FLY THERE?

SECURITY PROTOCOL, VERLOC! PROTECT THE EQUIPMENT. I DON'T KNOW WHAT STATE THOSE PEOPLE ARE IN AFTER FIVE YEARS ON THEIR OWN.

YEAH, YEAH.

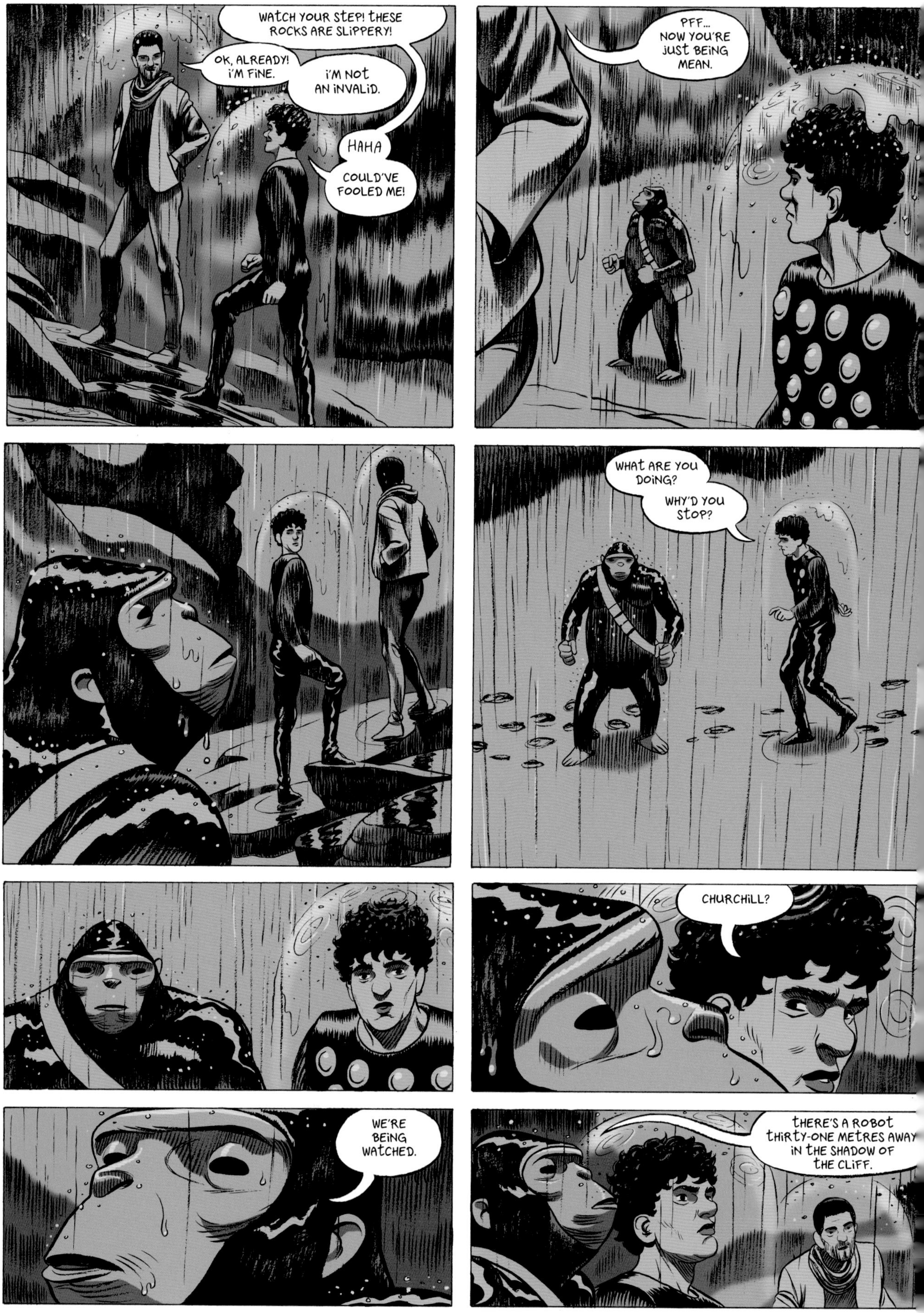
WATCH YOUR STEP! THESE ROCKS ARE SLIPPERY!
OK, ALREADY! I'M FINE.
I'M NOT AN INVALID.
HAHA
COULD'VE FOOLED ME!
PFF... NOW YOU'RE JUST BEING MEAN.
WHAT ARE YOU DOING?
WHY'D YOU STOP?
CHURCHILL?
WE'RE BEING WATCHED.
THERE'S A ROBOT THIRTY-ONE METRES AWAY IN THE SHADOW OF THE CLIFF.

MUST BE A ROBOT FROM THE COLONY.

PERFECTLY NORMAL.

HE IS IN COMBAT MODE.

COMBAT MODE?

WHAT FOR?

THERE'S NOTHING BUT MOLLUSCS AND A FEW COLONISTS ON THIS ROCK.

IS HE A DIRECT THREAT?

HE WILL NOT RISK ATTACKING ME ON HIS OWN.

CRAAK

LET'S KEEP MOVING.

WE'LL CLEAR THIS UP LATER.

KEEP AN EYE OUT!

45

I DIDN'T GET TO WRITE THIS TILL THE END OF THE FIRST DAY. IN HINDSIGHT, THE INCIDENT NOW SEEMS LIKE A CLEAR SIGN OF DANGER AHEAD. BUT AT THE TIME, I WASN'T FULLY IN REALITY YET — STILL LOST IN MY CHILDISH FANTASIES.

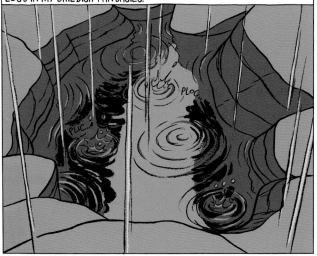

PLOC...

PLIC...

I FOUND THE INCIDENT VERY BEAUTIFUL AND EXCITING. I FELT PROTECTED. IT WAS ONLY THIS AFTERNOON, BUT HOW FAINT THE MEMORY ALREADY SEEMS...

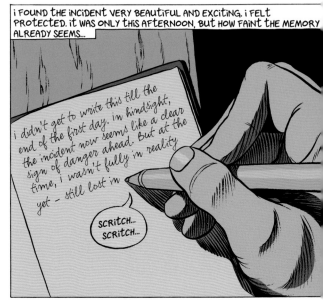

i didn't get to write this till the end of the first day. in hindsight, the incident now seems like a clear sign of danger ahead. But at the time, i wasn't fully in reality yet — still lost in

SCRITCH...
SCRITCH...

...FROM INSIDE THIS STONE CELL, NOW THAT MY EARS ARE RINGING AND MY HANDS ARE TREMBLING.

SOMETHING'S BEEN BOTHERING ME, VERLOC.

YES?

I HAVE TO EVALUATE THE RISKS OF BRINGING YOU ALONG, YOU UNDERSTAND.

STOP BEATING AROUND THE BUSH!

WHEN I SCRAPED YOU OFF THE STREET IN RADIANT, YOU HAD A NICE SHINER.

WHAT HAPPENED, EXACTLY?

SIGH

SILIKA LEFT ME FOR MANY REASONS. ONE WAS SHE'D FOUND ANOTHER GUY. A NICE, STAND-UP GUY, WORKED IN THE LAW DEPARTMENT OF A COMPANY WHERE SHE GAVE ENERGETIC MASSAGES TO DEPRESSED EXECS. ANYWAY...

THAT ASSHOLE CONVINCED HER TO DEPRIVE ME OF ALL VISITATION RIGHTS.

WHY?

WHY? WHY?!

BECAUSE I'M RESPONSIBLE FOR LILJA'S CONDITION, BULLSHIT LIKE THAT.

I MEAN, WHAT THE FUCK!

BUT THAT'S ANOTHER STORY.

THE MORNING YOU SCRAPED ME OFF THE STREET – AS YOU SO LOVINGLY PUT IT – I HADN'T SEEN LILJA IN ALMOST TWO MONTHS. THE NIGHT BEFORE, SHIA HADN'T BEEN ENOUGH TO DROWN MY SORROW AND RAGE.

SO I WENT OUT DETERMINED TO IGNORE THE COURT'S DECISION AND TALK TO HER. I KNEW I COULD CATCH HER AROUND TWENTY PAST EIGHT, WHEN SHE GOT TO THE INSTITUTE.

THE COURTYARD WAS AT THE BOTTOM OF A BIG FLIGHT OF STEPS. I SAW HER RIGHT AWAY FROM THE TOP.

SHE WAS WITH HER MOTHER.

ODDLY, I HAVE A VERY CLEAR MEMORY OF THEM, BUT AT THAT DISTANCE... THEY SHOULD HAVE BEEN A BLUR.

AND THEN MY HEART SCREECHED TO A HALT...

...WHEN SUDDENLY, FOR NO REASON AT ALL, SHE TURNED AROUND AND LOOKED RIGHT AT ME.

I ALSO SAW THERE WERE TWO MEN WITH HER. SILIKA SHOUTED SOMETHING AT THEM, AND THE TWO MEN STARTED TOWARD ME, BLOCKING MY WAY.

Reluha was!

MR. NIM! STOP!

THE LAW PROHIBITS YOUR COMING CLOSER.

C'MON, GUYS, RELAX! I KNOW YOU'RE JUST DOING YOUR JOB.

STOP! NOT ANOTHER STEP!

LET GO!

REMAIN CALM.

DON'T TOUCH ME, Y'HEAR?

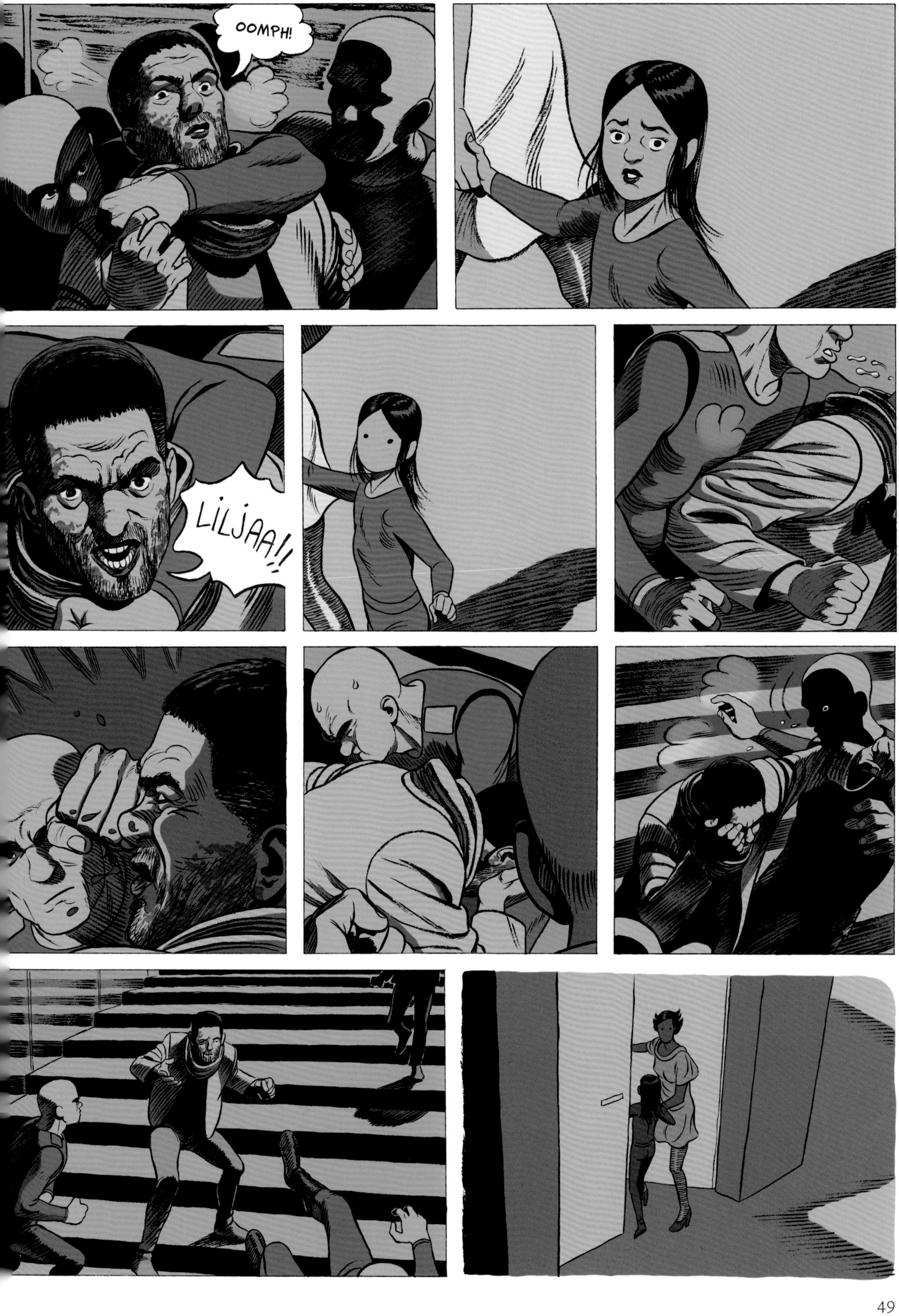

OOMPH!
LILJAA!!

I WOUND UP ESCAPING BEFORE THEY COULD REGROUP AND FINISH ME OFF.

IS THAT THE EXPLANATION YOU WANTED?

MM. EVERYTHING'S CLEARER NOW.

THANKS.

VERLOC?

WHAT NOW?

I—

HERE WE ARE!

SORRY TO INTERRUPT YOU.

BUT THE COLONY'S JUST AHEAD.

STILL NO RADIO SIGNAL?

NO. BUT THERE ARE SIGNS OF LIFE!

HOW MANY PEOPLE?

SIX DETECTED.

SHIT! THAT'S BAD!

THE MISSION HAD EIGHT MEMBERS.

WHAT ABOUT THE ROBOT?

HE'S MOVING, BUT STILL DISTANT.

YOU'RE HAPPY ABOUT ALL THIS, I CAN TELL.

IMMINENT ACTION ALWAYS DELIGHTS ME, MR. CONRAD!

I'D STARTED SWEATING FROM MY ARMPITS. I ALWAYS DO WHEN I'M NERVOUS. I REALIZED THERE WAS NO SHIA AROUND. NO WAY TO DROWN MY ANXIETY WHEN IT BROKE OUT.

WHAT THE FUCK WAS I DOING HERE? WHAT THE FUCK WAS I DOING HERE? THE QUESTION KEPT RUNNING ROUND MY SKULL.

I WANTED TO BE IN MY BED, AMONG MY BOOKS...

AHOY!

THIS LOOKS LIKE A BATTLEFIELD!

STAY WHERE YOU ARE!

NOT ANOTHER STEP!

MAGNETIC PULSE CANNON...

HOMEMADE...

DANGEROUS.

WHO ARE YOU?

MY NAME IS CONRAD NIM! I'M A REPRESENTATIVE OF THE MUY-TANG CORPORATION.

THIS IS MY ASSISTANT CHURCHILL, AND MY BROTHER, VERLOC NIM. BELIEVE ME, WE'RE HERE WITH THE BEST INTENTIONS.

PAH! SURE!

AFTER YEARS OF COMPLETE SILENCE, YOU SHOW UP ALL INNOCENT, OUT OF THE BLUE?

WITH THE BEST INTENTIONS?

PROVE IT!

I CAN SEND YOU MY ID FILES. BUT I'M NOT DETECTING ANY SIGNAL.

ALL YOUR IMPLANTS ARE OFFLINE.

GO AHEAD! HURRY UP!

BEEP

HM... YOUR CODES SEEM TO BE IN ORDER.

BEEP

YOU CAN TRUST US!

LET US IN!

TURN OFF YOUR ROBOT!

NO WAY! HE WORKS FOR ME!

I'LL VOUCH FOR HIM.

ROBOTS CAN'T BE TRUSTED AROUND HERE!

HE'S NOT LIKE OTHER ROBOTS.

HE MAY JUST BE THE BEST THING THAT'S HAPPENED TO YOU IN A LONG TIME!

VERY WELL.

BUT ONE FALSE MOVE, AND WE'LL DESTROY HIM!

KLUNK KLUNK KLUNK

AFTER YOU.

KLUNK KLUNK KLUNK

THEY'RE IN, MA'AM. WE'RE ON OUR WAY.

WHAT'S GOING ON HERE? WERE YOU ATTACKED?

WHAT'S GOING ON, MY DEAR SIR, IS THAT FIVE YEARS AGO YOU LEFT US HERE LIKE RATS IN A HOLE!

AND FIVE YEARS IS A LONG TIME WHEN YOU'RE ALL ALONE IN THE UNIVERSE.

I'M JUST A HUMBLE EMPLOYEE. I HAD NOTHING TO DO WITH IT.

OF COURSE. WE'RE ALL JUST HUMBLE EMPLOYEES.

YOU CAN BLAME THE GREAT CRISIS.

THE GREAT WHAT?

HM... LISTEN, I HAVE TO SEE PROFESSOR WOLAND.

KEEP MOVING! THERE IS NO PROFESSOR WOLAND ANY MORE! PROFESSOR WOLAND'S GONE!

ANOTHER DESERTER!

WELL? WHO ARE THEY?

MY DEAR MYO, IT SEEMS MUY-TANG HAS JUST REMEMBERED OUR EXISTENCE!

YOU THINK IT'S WISE TO LET A ROBOT IN?

ACCORDING TO OUR EMISSARY, HE'S NO ROBOT — HE'S GOOD NEWS!

HOW CAN WE AFFORD TO PASS UP SUCH A CHANCE?

HI THERE!

HELLO.

WHERE ARE YOU TAKING US?

THE LAB SECTION IS TOO EXPOSED.

WE HAVE TO GO DEEP INTO THE ROCK.

EXPOSED TO WHAT? HAVE YOU BEEN HAVING PROBLEMS WITH ROBOTS?

PROFESSOR KAPLAN WILL EXPLAIN EVERYTHING.

I REMEMBER SEEING CONRAD AND CHURCHILL EXCHANGE GLANCES AS WE WENT BY A CLOSED DOOR.

BREATH OF FRESH AIR, EH?

BUT THE SURPRISES JUST KEPT ON COMING.

WELCOME, WELCOME!

WELCOME? REALLY? WITH THESE GUNS TRAINED ON US?

TEE HEE! FORGIVE ME, IT WAS SARCASTIC.

YOU WOULD INDEED BE WELCOME WERE YOU BRINGING ANY HELP AT ALL... BUT IF YOU'RE JUST ANOTHER STAGE IN THIS ACCURSED TEST...

TEST? WHAT TEST?

DON'T PLAY GAMES WITH ME!

YOU CAME HERE ON FOOT. YOU TOOK CARE TO LAND YOUR SHIP FAR AWAY. PROTECT THE EQUIPMENT — AM I RIGHT? EQUIPMENT COMES FIRST! I KNOW YOUR PROTOCOLS, YOUNG MAN.

SO WHY ARE YOU HERE?

WHY... I'M ONLY HERE TO PREPARE THE GROUND.

HELP IS ON THE WAY!

IT TAKES SOME TIME TO GET A BIG INFRASTRUCTURE GOING, YOU KNOW. ESPECIALLY SINCE THE COMPANY'S STILL RECOVERING.

BUT IT'S ONLY A MATTER OF DAYS!

IT'S TIME FOR YOU TO GO HOME!

LIES! WHAT NERVE!

I SEE SOMEONE'S WOUNDED. I CAN HELP HIM RIGHT NOW, IF YOU'D LIKE.

DO YOU THINK I'M A MORON?

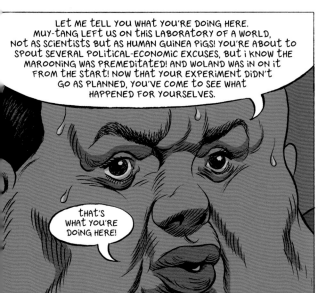

LET ME TELL YOU WHAT YOU'RE DOING HERE. MUY-TANG LEFT US ON THIS LABORATORY OF A WORLD, NOT AS SCIENTISTS BUT AS HUMAN GUINEA PIGS! YOU'RE ABOUT TO SPOUT SEVERAL POLITICAL-ECONOMIC EXCUSES, BUT I KNOW THE MAROONING WAS PREMEDITATED! AND WOLAND WAS IN ON IT FROM THE START! NOW THAT YOUR EXPERIMENT DIDN'T GO AS PLANNED, YOU'VE COME TO SEE WHAT HAPPENED FOR YOURSELVES.

THAT'S WHAT YOU'RE DOING HERE!

VERY WELL, THEN.

I SEE.

LISTEN, THERE'S BEEN A BIG MISUNDERSTANDING.

WANT ME TO BE HONEST WITH YOU?

I'LL BE FRANK.

KLIK

TELL YOUR GORILLA TO PUT OUT HIS CIGAR!

VRINK

PUFF

VERY IMPRESSIVE!

CHOMP CHOMP MUNCH

GOOD. NOW, HERE'S WHAT'S GOING TO HAPPEN.

WE'RE GOING DOWN TO THE LOCKED ROOM TO RETRIEVE WOLAND'S PRODUCT. THEN YOU'RE GOING TO LET US GO WITHOUT A FUSS, AND I PROMISE I'LL DO WHAT I CAN SO THAT MUY-TANG COMES FOR YOU AS SOON AS POSSIBLE.

AAMA!

SO THAT'S IT!

AAMA?!

DON'T TAKE THIS WRONG, BUT FOR A COMPANY REP, YOU'RE AN ODD DUCK.

UP TILL THEN, I WAS JUST A SPECTATOR – WORRIED, SURE, BUT NOT REALLY INVOLVED. BUT IT WAS LIKE THIS NEW REALITY HAD BEEN SECRETLY SAVING ME UP FOR A SPECIAL ROLE.

SUDDENLY, IT WAS MY TURN TO STEP ONSTAGE.

BEEP

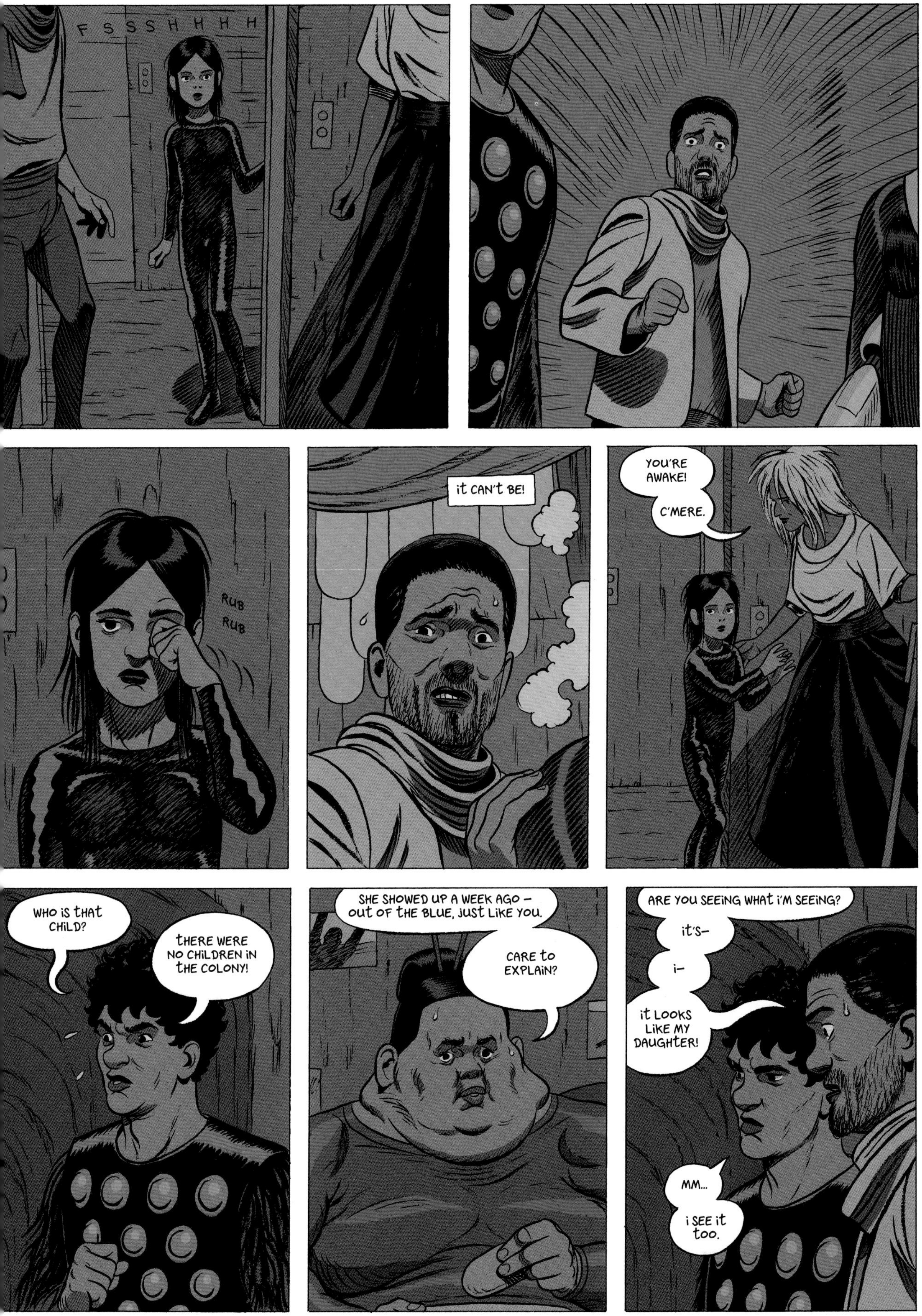
FSSSHHHH
RUB RUB
it CAN'T BE!
YOU'RE AWAKE!
C'MERE.
WHO iS THAT CHiLD?
THERE WERE NO CHILDREN iN THE COLONY!
SHE SHOWED UP A WEEK AGO – OUT OF THE BLUE, JUST LiKE YOU.
CARE TO EXPLAiN?
ARE YOU SEEiNG WHAT i'M SEEiNG?
iT'S–
i–
iT LOOKS LiKE MY DAUGHTER!
MM...
i SEE iT TOO.

BUT THIS IS IMPOSSIBLE! SHE'S ALMOST...

SHE LOOKS SO MUCH LIKE HER!

SAME HEIGHT... SAME HAIR...

ALMOST THE SAME EYES...

EEEEEEE

LILJA?

YOU'RE SCARING HER!

CONRAD, WHERE ARE WE?

WHAT'S GOING ON?

I DON'T KNOW.

BUT WE BETTER GET OUT FAST!

YOU TWO! WITH ME!

WE'RE HEADED DOWN FOR THE PRODUCT!

YOU WON'T FIND ANYTHING! WOLAND TOOK IT ALL!

IF YOUR ONLY MISSION WAS TO GET AAMA, SETTLE IN! YOU'LL BE HERE AWHILE! THAT GIVES US SOMETHING IN COMMON.

HOW UNEXPECTED.

SHOW ME, ANYWAY.

SHIT!

WE TOLD YOU SO!

THERE'S A TRANSPONDER ON THE POD BUT NOT THE INDIVIDUAL CYLINDERS, OF COURSE. STUPID MISTAKE!

WE HAVE A SERIOUS PROBLEM, CHURCHILL.

THINGS GET CLEARER AS THEY GO ON. OUR PRESENCE HERE ISN'T A SIMPLE COURTESY CALL. I'LL HAVE TO LIVE HERE FOR A WHILE. WITH THESE PEOPLE...

WITH HER.

THAT MUCH IS CLEAR.

AND I AM ALMOST RELIEVED.

PEOPLE, I'M THROUGH FOOLING AROUND!

I'M GOING TO MAKE MYSELF A LITTLE SNACK.

MEANWHILE, YOU FIGURE OUT HOW TO EXPLAIN WHAT HAPPENED IN THE LAST FIVE YEARS.

I DON'T HAVE A VERY CLEAR MEMORY OF WHAT WE ATE OR TALKED ABOUT. I WAS DISTRACTED, TO SAY THE LEAST.

THIS IS MORE OR LESS WHAT I PICKED UP: A FEW MONTHS AFTER SETTLING IN FIVE YEARS AGO, THE EIGHT COLONISTS SUDDENLY LOST ALL CONTACT WITH MUY-TANG.

TWO CAMPS SOON FORMED. THOSE LED BY PROFESSOR WOLAND BELIEVED SOME TECHNICAL OR POLITICAL PROBLEM HAD PUT THE PROJECT ON STANDBY, AND THEY SHOULD GO ON WITH THE EXPERIMENTS THEMSELVES.

THOSE LED BY PROFESSOR KAPLAN BELIEVED THAT THE RADIO SILENCE WAS PART OF A CALCULATED PLAN TO STUDY HOW THAT FAMOUS SOUP EVERYONE HERE CALLS AAMA WOULD CONTAMINATE EIGHT SCIENTISTS, AND IT WAS BETTER NOT TO START ANYTHING UNTIL MUY-TANG COULD BE REACHED.

THIS SECOND CAMP HELD THE UPPER HAND FOR A WHILE AS TENSIONS ROSE.

BUT RECENTLY, EVERYTHING STARTED HAPPENING VERY FAST, A CASCADE OF UNLIKELY EVENTS. ONE MORNING NINETY DAYS BEFORE WE ARRIVED, WOLAND LEFT WITH THE COVETED CYLINDERS. ABOUT A MONTH AGO, ALL THE ROBOTS – BUILDERS, ANALYZERS, EVERY MODEL BIG TO SMALL – VANISHED WITHOUT WARNING. SOME CAME BACK A FEW DAYS LATER AND DESTROYED A GOOD PART OF THE BASE'S TECH EQUIPMENT.

FINALLY, A WEEK AGO, THAT MYSTERIOUS LITTLE GIRL TURNED UP. NO ONE COULD EXPLAIN. THE SAME DAY, SHAKEN BY THE COINCIDENCE AND WORRIED FOR THEIR MENTOR WOLAND'S SURVIVAL, PROFESSORS RAJEEV AND GHO LEFT TO LOOK FOR HER. WHICH EXPLAINS WHY THREE COLONISTS ARE MISSING.

UNLIKELY EVENTS INDEED!

MUST'VE FELT STRANGE: YEARS WITHOUT INCIDENT, AND THEN...

HM.

ONE MIGHT SAY THIS DEFIES EVERY LAW OF PROBABILITY.

WHY DID YOU DEACTIVATE YOUR IMPLANTS?

AFTER THEIR ATTACKS, THE ROBOTS STARTED SCRAMBLING OUR INTERNAL NETWORKS.

PERSONALLY, I'D RATHER LIVE LIKE A PUROGENE THAN HAVE MY BRAINS FRIED!

FORGIVE ME, BUT...

HAVE YOU NO EXPLANATION FOR WOLAND'S DEPARTURE?

WELL, GO AHEAD, FULMINE! WHAT ARE YOU WAITING FOR? IT WON'T BE LONG BEFORE EVERYONE ABANDONS ME ANYWAY.

SIGH

THE DAY SHE LEFT, WOLAND GAVE US THIS.

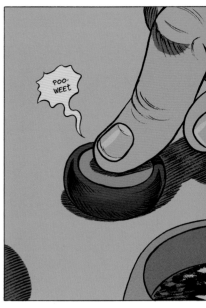

POO-WEET

DEAR FRIENDS.

I KNOW OF YOUR DOUBTS AND FEARS. I UNDERSTAND AND RESPECT THEM.

BUT I CAN'T HELP BUT BE SADDENED BY THE DEPLORABLE STATE OF OUR COMMUNITY RELATIONS, NOR CAN I HELP FEELING PARTLY RESPONSIBLE.

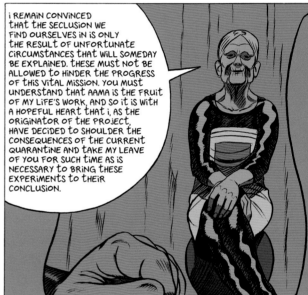

I REMAIN CONVINCED THAT THE SECLUSION WE FIND OURSELVES IN IS ONLY THE RESULT OF UNFORTUNATE CIRCUMSTANCES THAT WILL SOMEDAY BE EXPLAINED. THESE MUST NOT BE ALLOWED TO HINDER THE PROGRESS OF THIS VITAL MISSION. YOU MUST UNDERSTAND THAT AAMA IS THE FRUIT OF MY LIFE'S WORK, AND SO IT IS WITH A HOPEFUL HEART THAT I, AS THE ORIGINATOR OF THE PROJECT, HAVE DECIDED TO SHOULDER THE CONSEQUENCES OF THE CURRENT QUARANTINE AND TAKE MY LEAVE OF YOU FOR SUCH TIME AS IS NECESSARY TO BRING THESE EXPERIMENTS TO THEIR CONCLUSION.

SO I WILL BORROW A SURVEYOR AND ENOUGH STORES FROM THE BASE TO SURVIVE FOR A FEW MONTHS...

AND HEAD FAR AWAY, FOR THE ERZULIE SWAMPS, TO FREE AAMA AND LET IT FULFILL THE DESTINY FOR WHICH IT WAS CONCEIVED.

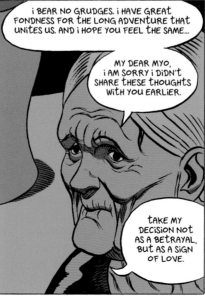

I BEAR NO GRUDGES. I HAVE GREAT FONDNESS FOR THE LONG ADVENTURE THAT UNITES US. AND I HOPE YOU FEEL THE SAME...

MY DEAR MYO, I AM SORRY I DIDN'T SHARE THESE THOUGHTS WITH YOU EARLIER.

TAKE MY DECISION NOT AS A BETRAYAL, BUT AS A SIGN OF LOVE.

DON'T TRY TO FOLLOW ME. IT'LL ONLY MAKE THINGS WORSE.

YOUR FRIEND...

GOODBYE.

POO-WEET

WHERE ARE THE ERZULIE SWAMPS?

?!

WII WII WII WII WII

WII WII

WHAT IS THAT?

THE ALARM FOR THE MAIN DOOR!

THIS IS WHAT HAPPENS WHEN WE LET OUR GUARD DOWN!

WIIWIIW

WII WII

WHERE'S THE GIRL?

THE ROBOT'S RIGHT BELOW US.

GIVE US BACK OUR GUNS!

STAY CALM. WE'LL HANDLE THIS.

DO SOMETHING, YOU FOOL!

THE GIRL? WHERE'S THE GIRL?

I... I THINK SHE WENT DOWNSTAIRS EARLIER...

WAIT!

SHIT!

HERE, TAKE THIS!

WHAT?

YOU CRAZY?

WHAT DO I DO WITH THIS?

BETTER YOU THAN ONE OF THEM.

LET'S GO!

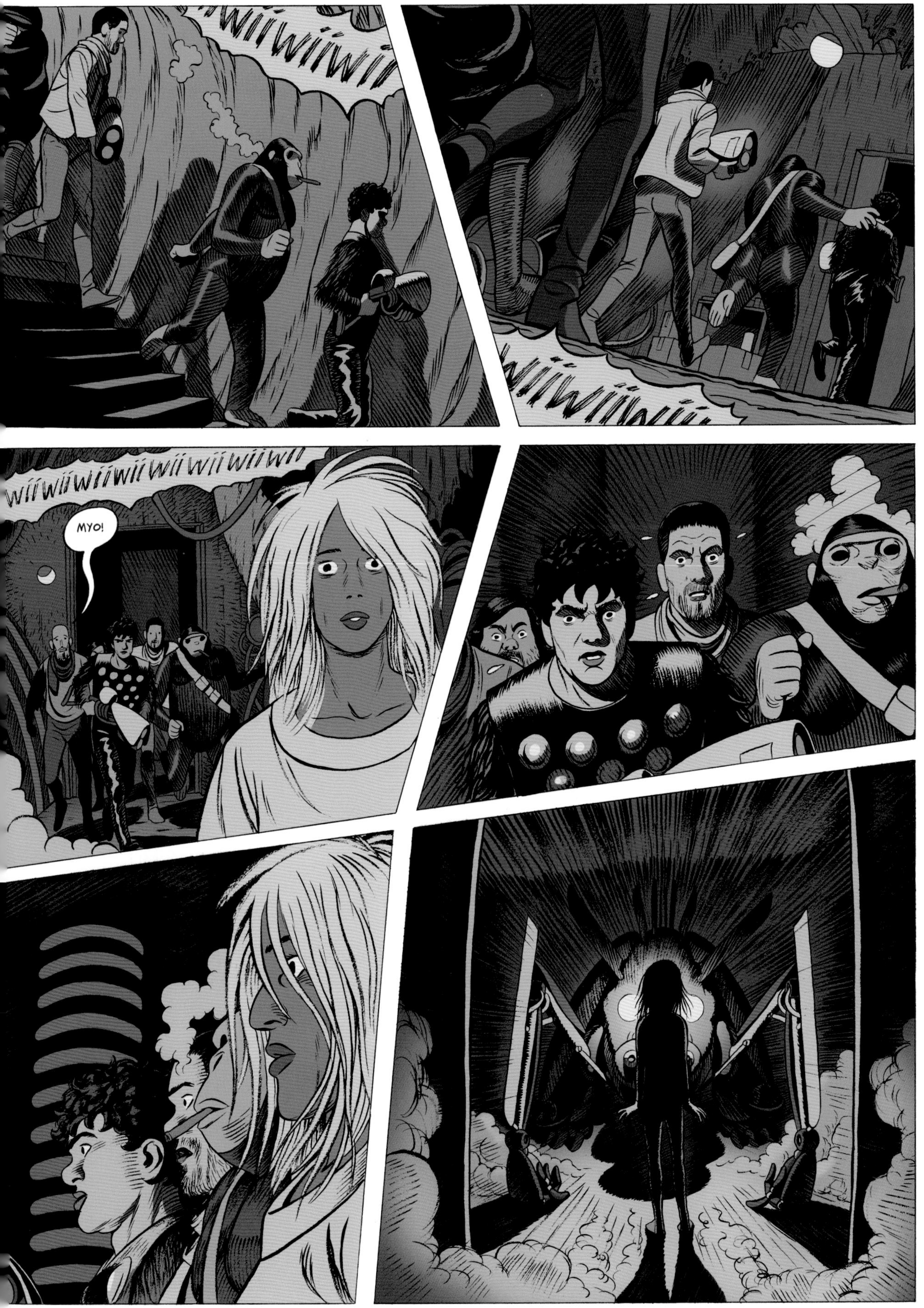
WIIWIIWIIWII
WIIWIIWIIWII
WIIWIIWIIWIIWIIWIIWIIWIIWII
MYO!

DON'T MAKE ANY SUDDEN MOVES!

BZZt

CHURCHILL!

WHATEVER IT TAKES.

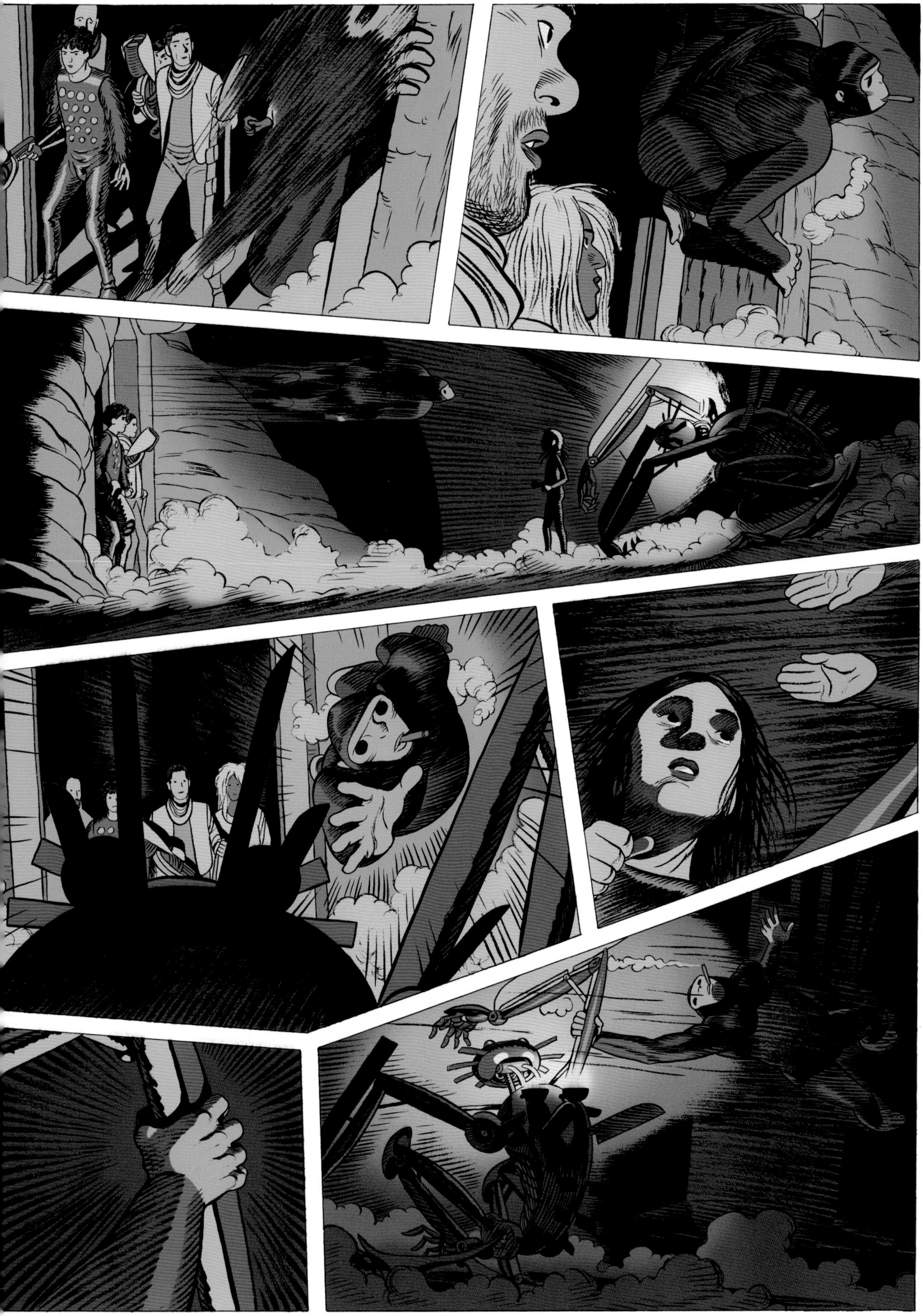

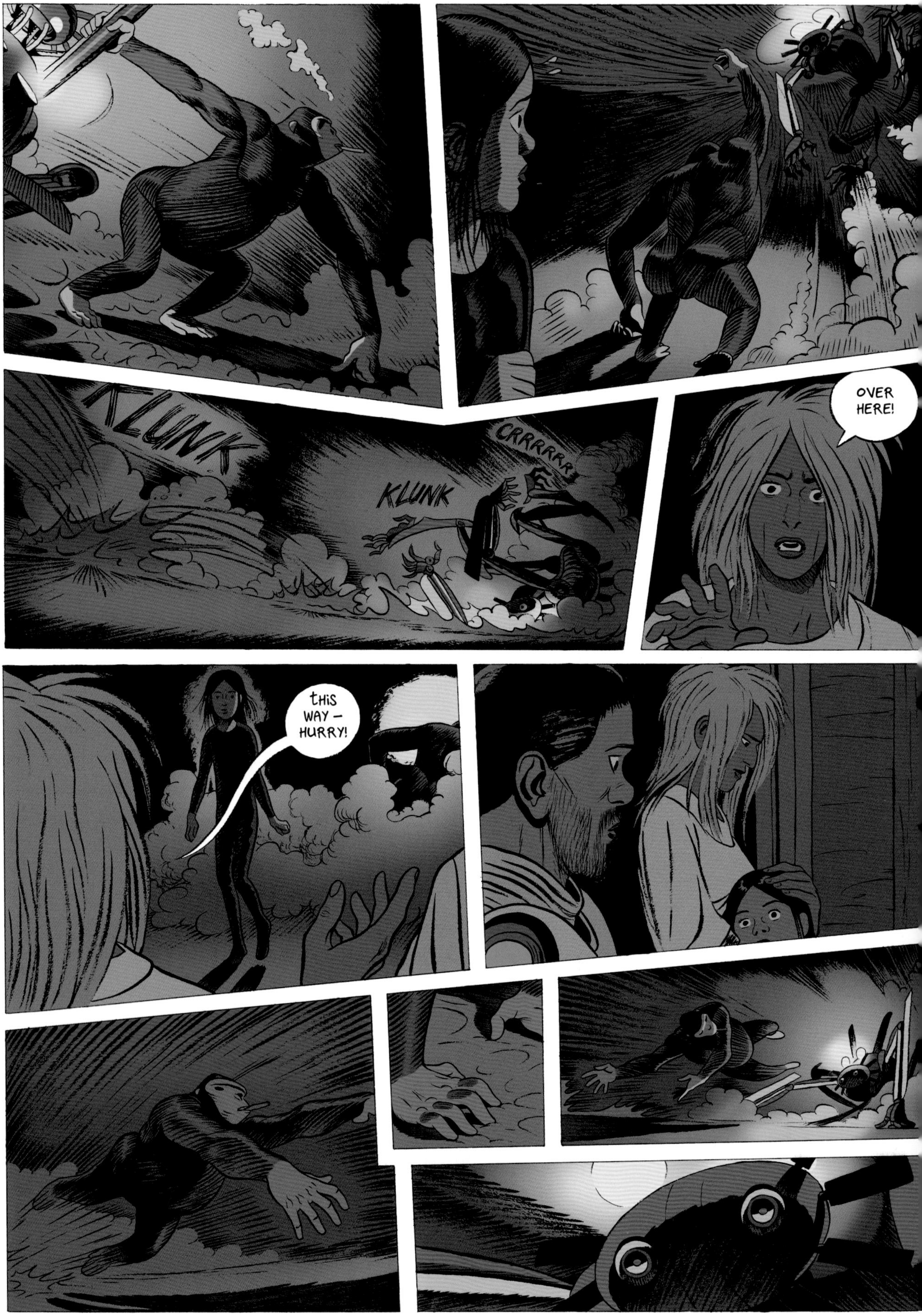

KLUNK
CRRRRRR
KLUNK
OVER HERE!
THIS WAY – HURRY!

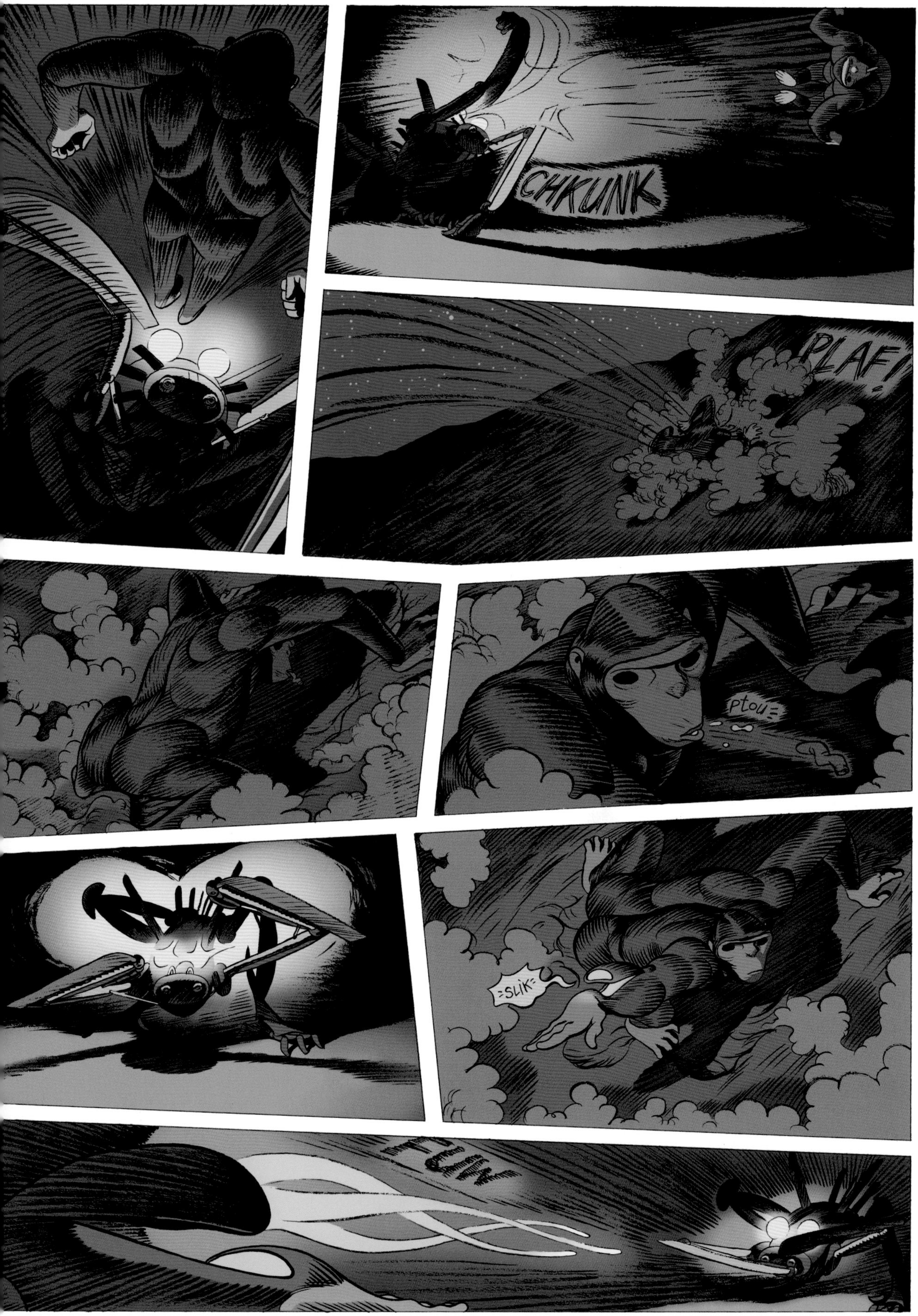
CHKUNK
PLAF!
ptou
SLIK

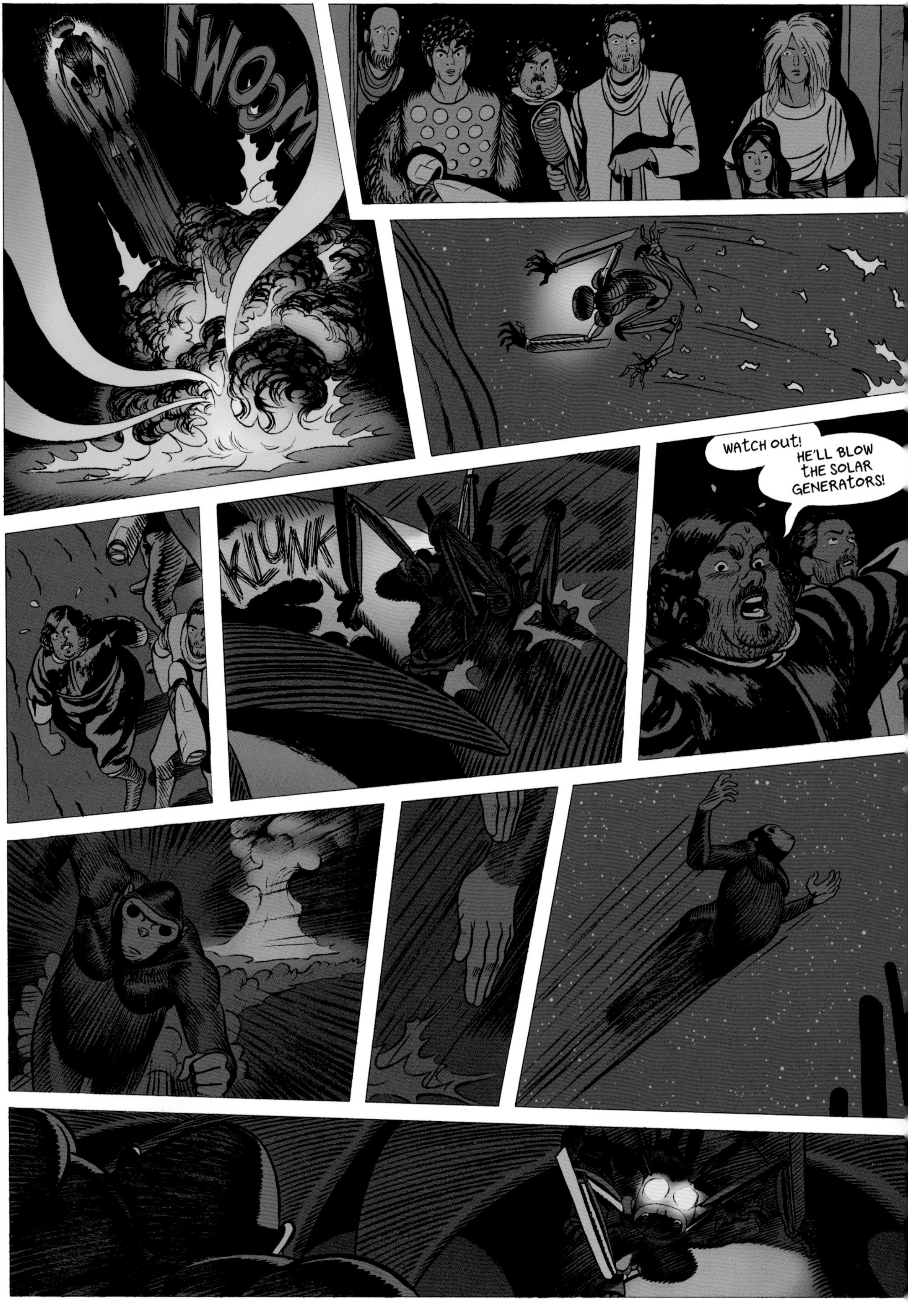
FWOOOM
WATCH OUT!
HE'LL BLOW THE SOLAR GENERATORS!
KLUNK!

ACTUALLY... I'VE NEVER HAD A CLOSER BRUSH WITH DEATH. NOT THAT MY LIFE WAS REALLY IN DANGER, BUT I'D NEVER PHYSICALLY EXPERIENCED SUCH UNCHECKED VIOLENCE. SO QUICK, AND SO VICIOUS!

I CAN STILL FEEL THE HEAT OF IT ON MY FACE...

HE FINALE WAS LIKE A BLURRY, FAR-OFF FIREWORKS HOW.

I FELT HER JUMP AT THE SECOND EXPLOSION, BRUSHING AGAINST THE BACK OF MY HAND.

I WAS DAZZLED BY THE VISION OF THOSE TWIN COMETS CRASHING INTO THE OPPOSITE CLIFF.

POWF!

LET'S GET BACK UNDER SHELTER.

BUT... WHAT ABOUT YOUR ROBOT?

DON'T WORRY.

THIS IS HIS IDEA OF FUN.

?!!

AH, YOU'RE JUST IN TIME.

I WANT A COMPLETE RUNDOWN OF THAT THING'S MEMORY.

RIGHT AWAY!

THINGS EVENTUALLY CALMED DOWN AFTER THE SHOCK. A LONG CONVERSATION PUT US AT EASE AND LET EVERYONE GET BETTER ACQUAINTED.

AND SO I FOUND OUT THAT FULMINE IS A BIOROBOTICS RESEARCHER. HE'S CLEARLY IN PROFESSOR KAPLAN'S THRALL, OBEYS HER EVERY WHIM. TO THE OTHERS, HE'S KIND OF A FIRST SECRETARY, A DELEGATE TO THE ORGANIZATION. HE THINKS OF PILGRIMM AS HIS DOCILE ASSISTANT.

PILGRIMM HIMSELF IS A MATHS AND COMPUTER WHIZ. AND AS SLIPPERY AS HE IS SILENT. I CAUGHT HIM SNEAKING FEVERISH GLANCES AT MYO MORE THAN ONCE. NO HASTY CONCLUSIONS. OUR ARRIVAL SEEMS TO HAVE GREATLY DISTURBED HIM.

MYO IS A BIOTECH PROFESSOR. SHE'S WOLAND'S DISCIPLE, ALMOST A DAUGHTER TO HER. HER ASSERTIVE YET INTROSPECTIVE NATURE GIVES HER A POTENT CHARM. BUT THE OTHER COLONISTS SEEM TO KEEP HER AT A DISTANCE.

THE ONE I KNOW LEAST ABOUT IS DOCTOR FRIENKO. HE'S A PHYSICIAN. THE WOUND IN HIS ARM IS FROM THE LAST ROBOT ATTACK. AT ONE POINT, FULMINE CALLED HIM "OUR BLOND ANGEL", WITH A HINT OF ACERBITY.

PROFESSOR KAPLAN CAN SEEM BITTER, PARANOID AND OUTRAGEOUSLY VORACIOUS. HER HOLD ON THE OTHERS COMES FROM MANIPULATION AND EMOTIONAL BLACKMAIL. BUT I MUST BEWARE OF SNAP JUDGMENTS. JUST NOW, BEFORE OUR LITTLE MEETING, I HAD AN ENDEARING SURPRISE.

!?!

AM I DREAMING?

IS THAT... IS THAT A LITTLE BIBLE YOU HAVE THERE?

GET AWAY!

YOU KNOW THAT ACCORDING TO RECENT RELIGIOUS LEGISLATION, YOU'RE AN OUTLAW?

I'M NOT RELIGIOUS.

IT'S JUST A FAMILY HEIRLOOM.

HOW REVERENTLY YOU READ YOUR FAMILY HEIRLOOM!

IT COMFORTS ME. IS THAT ILLEGAL?

IT'S AN EXCELLENT WAY OF KEEPING A FEW THINGS CLEAR AMIDST CHAOS.

AND YOU'D BE SURPRISED BY THE SIMILARITIES TO BE FOUND BETWEEN OUR SITUATION AND THAT OF THE CHOSEN PEOPLE...

IF THAT MEANS ANYTHING TO YOU.

YOU HAVE NO IDEA...

ARE YOU GOING TO TELL ON ME?

I'D NEVER TELL ON ANYONE FOR READING A BOOK!

PERISH THE THOUGHT!

MAY I HAVE A LOOK?

OUT OF THE QUESTION!

UH, WELL...

PARDON ME.

I'LL LEAVE YOU TO IT.

YOU'RE AN ODD ONE.

I DON'T KNOW WHAT YOU'RE DOING HERE.

YOU'RE LIKE A FISH OUT OF WATER.

COULD BE THAT, BENEATH AN UNPLEASANT EXTERIOR, THAT WOMAN ND I ARE VERY SIMILAR. I'M NOT RULING IT OUT.

AS FOR THE GIRL: MOST OF THE TIME SHE SEEMS A PRISONER OF HER OWN BODY, OF A SENSORY AUTARCHY.

MYO SAYS SHE'S MUTE...

...LIKE LILJA.

NO MORE FOR TODAY.

I'LL STOP HERE FOR NOW.

FASCINATING AS IT WAS, CHURCHILL'S LITTLE SHOW HAS LEFT ME FEELING DIZZY.

I'LL TRY TO GET SOME SLEEP.

MAYBE LEAVE THE LIGHT ON...

CHURCHILL?

YES?

JUDGING FROM THE NUMBER OF PAGES I HAVE LEFT TO READ, IT'LL TAKE US SEVERAL DAYS TO GET BACK TO THE COLONY.

PROBABLY.

WHAT DO YOU MEAN, PROBABLY?

IT IS DIFFICULT TO ESTIMATE. WE DID NOT COME ALL THIS WAY ON FOOT.

AND THE ENVIRONS HAVE CHANGED SO MUCH...

I JUST READ ABOUT YOUR BATTLE WITH THE COLONY ROBOT... DON'T YOU HAVE SOMETHING THAT'LL SAVE US SOME TIME?

NOT IN THIS STATE, NO.

WAIT, THE BUZZING'S STARTING AGAIN...

STRONGER THAN BEFORE.

WE HAVE NO CHOICE. WE MUST KEEP MOVING.

THE VESSEL WILL SOON BE ENTERING APPROACH PHASE.

JUST A MINUTE!

AS IF THE GROUND WERE WHISPERING TO MY FEET.

WHAT IF IT WERE A LANGUAGE?

A CALL?

I UNDERSTAND...

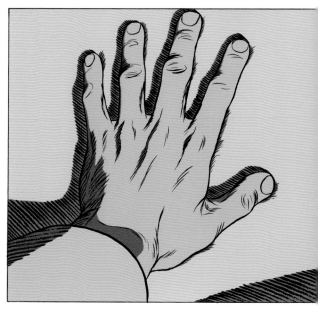

80

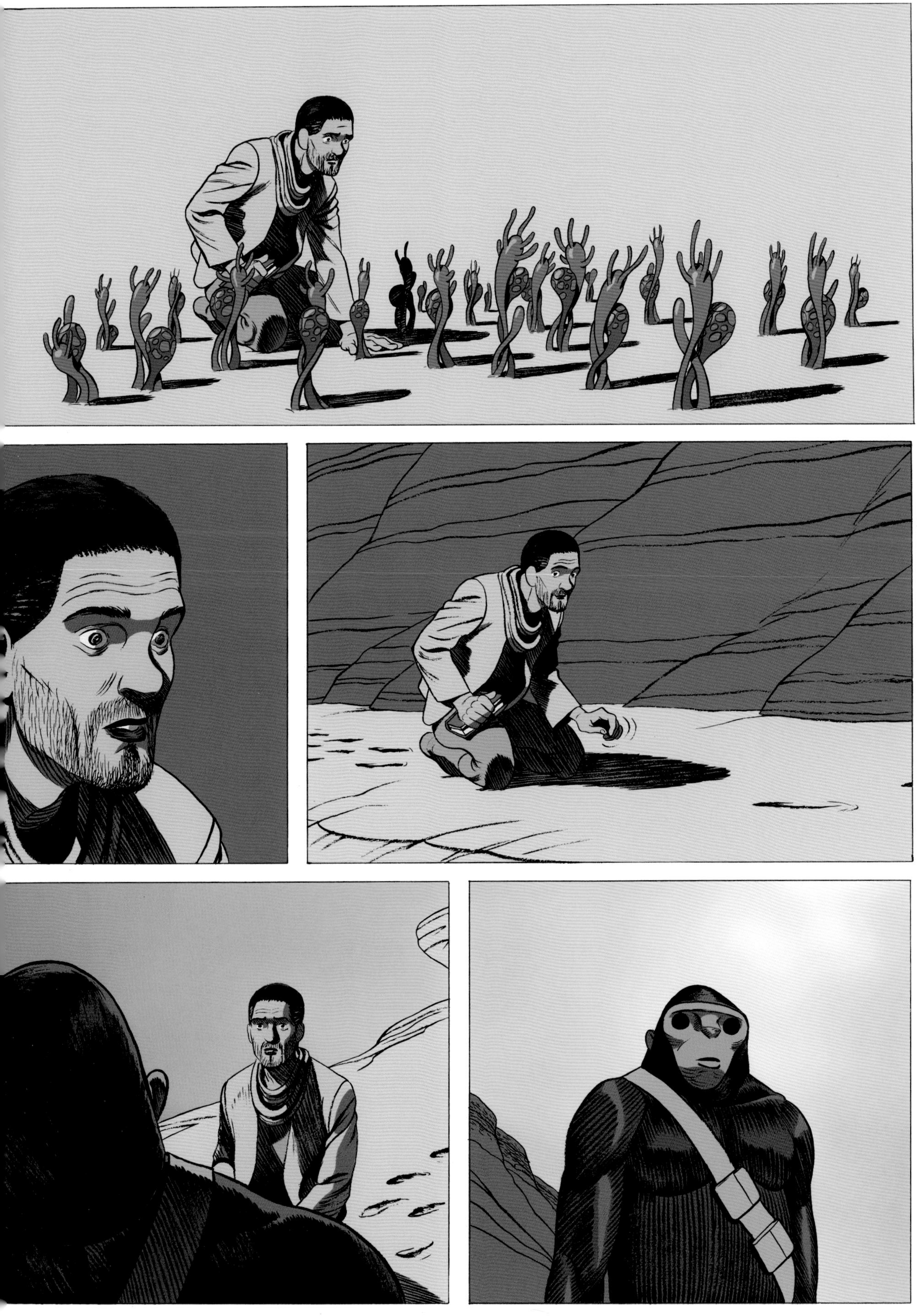

I MUST ADD A POSTSCRIPT TO MY RECORD OF THIS DAY. WHAT JUST HAPPENED IS TOO INCREDIBLE. JUST AS I WAS GOING TO BED, THERE WAS A KNOCK AT THE DOOR.

KNOCK KNOCK

IT'S OPEN!

IT WAS MYO. BUT SHE WAS DIFFERENT...

SSSSSSS

AM I BOTHERING YOU?

DISHEVELLED...

NO, NO, I WAS ABOUT TO—

THERE'S SOMETHING I REALLY HAVE TO TELL YOU.

SURE, ABSOLUTELY — HAVE A SEAT?

NO.

YOU'RE PROBABLY GOING LOOKING FOR WOLAND AND AAMA TOMORROW, RIGHT?

OH, THAT. WELL, I CAN'T SAY.

CONRAD AND CHURCHILL MUST BE DECIDING RIGHT NOW.

BUT YOU'RE RIGHT — THERE'S A GOOD CHANCE.

SUDDENLY SHE LOOKED TENSE, ALMOST TERRIFIED. HER EYES SHONE.

A BEAT...

IS EVERYTHING OK?

YOU WANTED TO TELL ME SOMETHING?

YES, YES...

I...

"SIGH"

I DON'T KNOW WHY I'M FIGHTING IT.

IT'S RIDICULOUS.

FIGHTING WHAT, PROFESSOR?

i KNEW QUITE WELL. BUT THANKS TO MY SHYNESS, i'M GOOD AT PLAYING FAUX-NAÏVE.

CALL ME MYO!

IN FACT, FEMALE DESIRE TERRIFIES ME. RATHER, WHAT TERRIFIES ME IS THE VIOLENT AROUSAL IT PROVOKES IN ME.

MY STOMACH KNOTS AND MY PULSE POUNDS AT MY TEMPLES...

SORRY?

i'M NOT ONE OF THOSE GIRLS!

DON'T GET ME WRONG!

IT'S... IT'S BECAUSE OF THE IMPLANTS!

BUT SOON i FELT DUTY-BOUND TO PLAY IT COOL, CONFIDENT AND – HOPEFULLY – VIRILE...

NO NEED TO APOLOGIZE.

i DON'T KNOW... EVER SINCE WE UNPLUGGED OUR IMPLANTS, IT'S REALLY MESSED WITH MY HORMONES.

AND ALL THE GUYS HERE ARE SO...

WEIRD...

YEAH, i KNOW.

i WENT THROUGH THE SAME THING WHEN i GOT RID OF MY OWN IMPLANTS.

BUT THE EFFECT SOON WEARS OFF.

YOU GOT R–!

WITHOUT HAVING TO?

i HAVE A VERY ORIGINAL VISION OF LIFE.

SO WE'RE LIKE TWO MYSTERIOUS SAVAGES ABANDONED TO OUR BASEST INSTINCTS...

WHY SO MANY THINGS IN A SINGLE DAY? SHOULD I HAVE DEPRIVED MYSELF OF A MOMENT LIKE THIS?

IT'S A BIT LATE TO WONDER NOW...

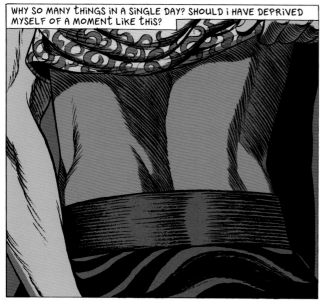

I WAS COMPLETELY FAITHFUL TO SILIKA IN ALL THE YEARS WE WERE TOGETHER. EVEN WHEN THINGS STARTED TO FALL APART AND HEAD SOUTH.

AFTER THAT, I MIGHT HAVE FANTASIZED ABOUT A CUSTOMER OFFERING HERSELF TO ME IN THE SHOP'S BACK ROOM. BUT I MUST ADMIT, I MOSTLY MADE DO WITH IMAGINARY EROTIC FLIGHTS OF FANCY BROUGHT ON BY THE SHIA...

SO, NO, I DON'T REGRET IT! IT WAS AN INTENSE AND ROMANTIC EXPERIENCE. EVEN IF I SOON REALIZED THAT HORMONAL UPSET WASN'T THE ONLY REASON FOR HER UNEXPECTED DRIVES.

YOU'RE GOING TO NEED ME.

WHAT FOR?

FOR YOUR EXPEDITION. TAKE ME WITH YOU. I KNOW WOLAND BEST. I WAS THERE WHEN AAMA WAS CREATED.

YOU HAVE NO IDEA WHAT YOU'RE GOING TO FIND.

I HAVE NO SAY IN ALL THAT. I'M JUST ALONG FOR THE RIDE, YOU KNOW.

BUT YOU COULD TALK TO YOUR BROTHER!

HAH!

SO THAT'S IT!

YOU THINK I THREW MYSELF AT YOU JUST SO YOU'D ASK YOUR BROTHER TO BRING ME ALONG?

AS IT TURNS OUT, I'M ALSO QUITE GOOD AT ACTUALLY BEING NAÏVE.

UH, NO...

AND YOU'D LEAVE ALL YOUR FRIENDS HERE BEHIND JUST LIKE THAT?

THEY'RE A BUNCH OF WILLFUL CHILDREN! THEY COMPLETELY BOTCHED THE PROJECT WITH THEIR EGOTISTICAL QUARRELS.

AND I CAN'T STAND CRAZY OLD KAPLAN!

REALLY?

SHE DOESN'T SEEM THAT INSANE TO ME.

HER PERSONALITY TOOK A NOSEDIVE AFTER WE LOST CONTACT.

SHE STARTED EATING FOR TWELVE.

TO "COMPENSATE", SHE SAID.

ALL BECAUSE HER DADDY ABANDONED HER WHEN SHE WAS SEVEN.

AND THEN SHE FORCED HER NIGHTLY READINGS OF RELIGIOUS MYTH ON US, LIKE CHILDREN BEFORE BEDTIME.

SHE SAYS IT BRINGS US CLOSER TOGETHER.

YEAH, RIGHT!

I LET WOLAND GO.

THEN RAJEEV, WHO TOOK SUCH GOOD CARE OF ME.

I CAN'T STAY HERE AND WAIT.

WILL YOU HELP ME?

CONRAD'S VERY PROUD. HE HATES FEELING MANIPULATED.

YOU'D BE BETTER OFF ASKING HIM YOURSELF.

I'LL DO WHAT I CAN TO BACK YOU UP.

to be continued...

FREDERIK AVR 20